# TILLINGBOURNE

## The Tillingbourne Bus Story

George Burnett & Laurie James

*Front Cover -*

Demonstrating the extremes of the British climate are two Bedford YRQ buses with well-finished Plaxton Derwent bodywork, which typified the Tillingbourne fleet in the late 1970s.

(Top) GPA 846 N is seen on a fine Summer Sunday working the Scenic Circular service, out of its then normal area passing through the village of Hascombe. Since 1986, however, Tillingbourne has been the only provider of a regular bus service for Hascombe. (K.Newton)

(Bottom) MPE 248 P waits at the Farley Green terminus on a cold Saturday morning. Some of Tillingbourne's rural routes rarely see snow clearance, and this was the first time for two days that a bus had managed to reach the village. Both vehicles were sold in the early 1980s and saw further bus service in Surrey. (G.Burnett)

*Back Cover -*

(Top) Tillingbourne was well known for its fleet of maroon liveried ex-London Transport Guy GS buses, however less known was ex-GS 64, MXX 364, the last such vehicle purchased from London Country Bus Services and one of the first in the fleet to be painted in the Danube blue, light grey and yellow livery soon to become so familiar, here working the Farley Green service. (K.Newton)

(Bottom) If one discounts the Reigate - Leigh Postbus, in 1986 Tillingbourne was the first independent operator to work a local bus service in Reigate since the 1920s when Arthur Henry Hawkins' East Surrey Company achieved a monopoly of local bus operation there. So popular were the new 547/587 services that some journeys soon needed a larger vehicle than the 21 seat Iveco minibuses bought specially for the routes. The first of several Lex Maxeta bodied small Bedfords acquired was B919 NPC, which, unlike the subsequent purchases, was painted into Hobbit livery. It is anticipated that sister vehicle B918 NPC will enter service in Reigate during 1990. (Authors Collection)

*First published June 1990*

*ISBN 0 906520 77 0*



*Design - Deborah Goodridge*

*Published by Middleton Press*
*Easebourne Lane*
*Midhurst, West Sussex*
*GU29 9AZ*
*Tel. (0730) 813169*

*Printed & bound by Biddles Ltd,*
*Guildford and Kings Lynn*

# CONTENTS



# MAPS

# PREFACE

Tillingbourne Valley Services Ltd. was a typical small independent bus company operating stage carriage services in a very scenically-attractive part of rural west Surrey. It was well known both in the transport industry in general, and especially to the bus enthusiast, having survived the threat of absorption in 1933 by the all-embracing London Transport and having safely passed through a hiatus period in the late 1960s and early 1970s when its survival was very much in doubt. Subsequently, the Company changed hands and, as the local state owned undertakings were forced to contract their rural operations, Tillingbourne expanded, culminating in the radical enlargement of its share of the local bus market in 1985, which has been built upon since the implementation of "Deregulation" in October 1986. In recent years the Company has been, on occasions, the first to take delivery of new vehicle models, and this, coupled with the doctrines pursued by the energetic management, has kept Tillingbourne in the limelight of the media, and the Company has been held up as an example of successful independent bus operation. Now that provincial bus companies are outside state control, Tillingbourne has held its place in the new operating environment and still commands respect from competitors and loyalty from its regular passengers.

Much has appeared in print in recent years about Tillingbourne's activities and, to celebrate the Company's Golden Jubilee in 1974, its manager wrote a brief descriptive history. Now, fifteen years later, the Company has grown out of all recognition, and the authors felt that a comprehensive illustrated definitive history of Tillingbourne was needed.

As always, with a work which details the pre-war history of a bus operator, it has proved impossible to clarify all dates, and the background to some of the events has been lost in the mists of time. It is hoped that there are not too many ommisions or errors, but, unfortunately, evidence or witness of the Company's formative years is sparse or, when available, often contradictory. However, it is hoped that some of the flavour of Tillingbourne's operations is conveyed in these words and pictures and that the reader will be tempted to sample the current bus services and see the Valley of the Tillingbourne at first hand.

# INTRODUCTION

Surveying the Surrey countryside south east of the county town of Guildford today, it is hard to comprehend that the small Tillingbourne chalk-stream should have been responsible for the narrow, deep sided valley that runs eastwards from the River Wey near Guildford towards Dorking. Guildford, being situated some 30 miles from London at a strategic gap in the North Downs, has ancient origins resulting from being a focal point for road, and later rail, communications. The modern Anglican Cathedral and the University of Surrey are now as much symbols of Guildford as the steep cobbled High Street with its famous clock.

The town has always been a commercial and shopping centre for a large hinterland, and now its expanding housing estates provide homes for many London commuters. To the east rise the Surrey Hills, with views across the Downs to the popular beauty spot and viewpoint at Newlands Corner and the Tillingbourne Valley beyond.

The River Tillingbourne rises on the northern slopes of Leith Hill, which at 967 feet above sea-level is the highest point in the south eastern counties, and its fast flowing clear waters meander through the villages of Abinger, Gomshall, Shere, Albury and Chilworth before meeting the Wey near Shalford. Shere, with its ancient cottages and weeping willows fringing the river, is always popular with visitors, as is the nearby peaceful Silent Pool. The water power of the Tillingbourne has been harnessed in the past for milling and iron-forging purposes, and was employed by Gomshall Tannery until very recently. This is said to be one of the oldest tanneries in England. At Chilworth there was once a papermill producing paper for banknotes and also a gunpowder plant established in about 1625 by the East India Company. The latter two industries were described, on one of his rural rides, as "most damnable purposes" by the early 19th century travel writer, William Cobbett, himself hailing from the nearby town of Farnham. Although industry no longer needs the Tillingbourne, the river still plays a vital role. Every day, between 4 and 7 million gallons of water are extracted from the Tillingbourne by Shalford Pumping Station from a total flow of 12 million gallons, and thus most of the population of Godalming and half of that of Guildford, approximately 150,000 people in total, rely on the Tillingbourne for their supply of fresh water.

A railway line through the Tillingbourne Valley was opened in 1849, with stations at Shalford, Chilworth and Gomshall. It was originally worked by the South Eastern Railway (from 1899, the South Eastern and Chatham Railway) and formed part of a cross-country route from Reading to Guildford, Dorking, Redhill and Tonbridge. Diesel multiple units were introduced by British Rail in 1965 to replace steam haulage. The station at Shalford is situated in the centre of the village, but those at Gomshall and Chilworth are some way from the main settlements. The full story of this railway line is told in "Guildford to Redhill" (Middleton Press). At Guildford and Dorking the stations are a little way from the shopping areas, so there was plenty of potential for a local bus service. Network SouthEast currently has proposals to electrify the Reading to Gatwick line, and if this is successful Shalford Station may be developed as a park and ride point, hopefully resulting in the reduction of some of Guildford's peak hour traffic congestion.

More important from the point of view of this account, Chilworth was the home village of George Trice. Trice was a builder by profession and had been a foreman at the gunpowder factory until its closure in 1920. At the peak of its activities during the First World War, over 600 workers produced cordite for munitions at the factory. The workers paid a regular subscription into a fund so that they could be paid in the event of illness or injury, and George Trice was known locally as the man who administered this fund. As a builder, amongst the houses he constructed locally were several in New Road, Chilworth. It is said that he also ran a horse-drawn carriers wagon which was used mainly for delivering goods but also carried a few passengers into Guildford.

## Tillingbourne Valley Services
1924 - 1970

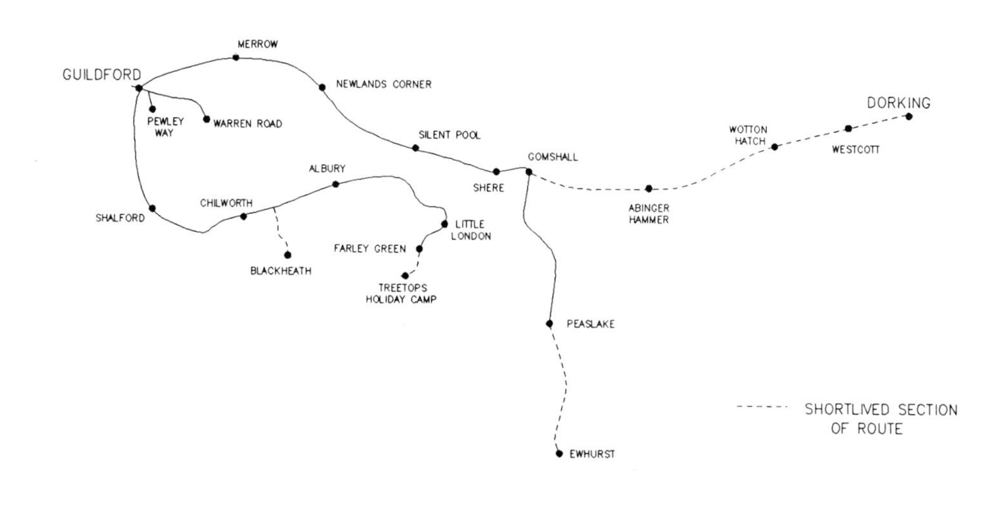


## Tillingbourne Orpington Area Services
March 1981 - September 1983

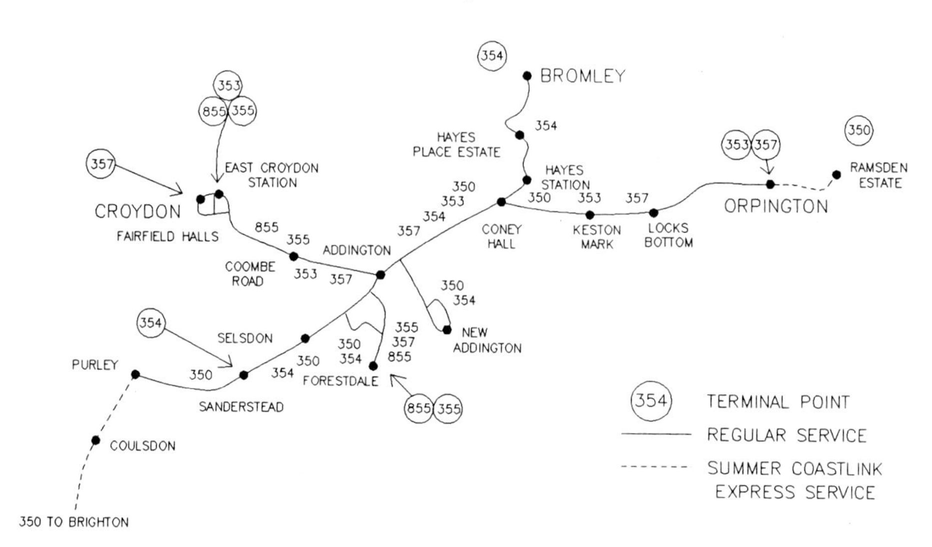

## Tillingbourne Surrey & Sussex Services
October 1970 - June 1982

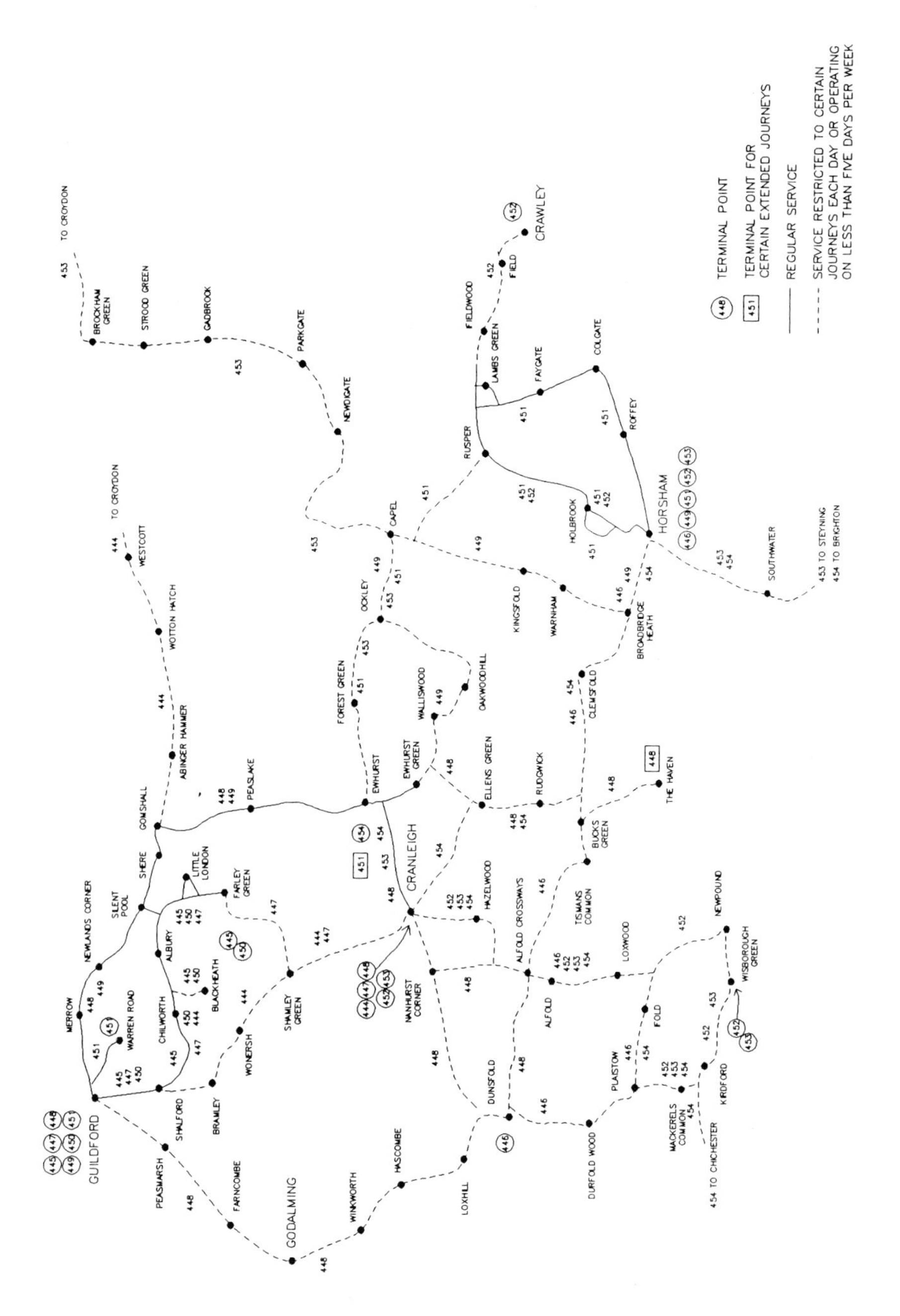

## Tillingbourne Surrey & Sussex Services
July 1982 - March 1985

(448) TERMINAL POINT

——— REGULAR SERVICE

- - - - - SERVICE RESTRICTED TO CERTAIN JOURNEYS EACH DAY (e.g. SCHOOL JOURNEYS) OR OPERATING ON LESS THAN FIVE DAYS PER WEEK.

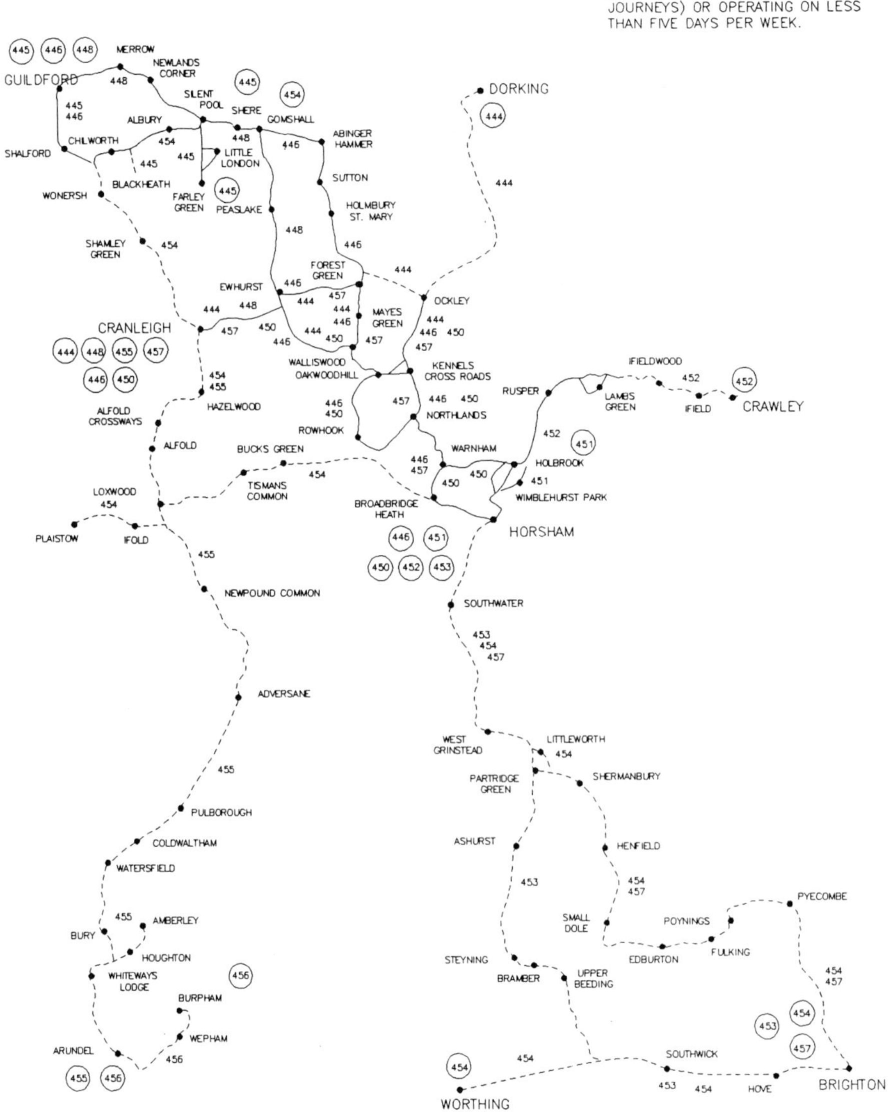

## Tillingbourne Surrey & Sussex Services
April 1985 - October 1986

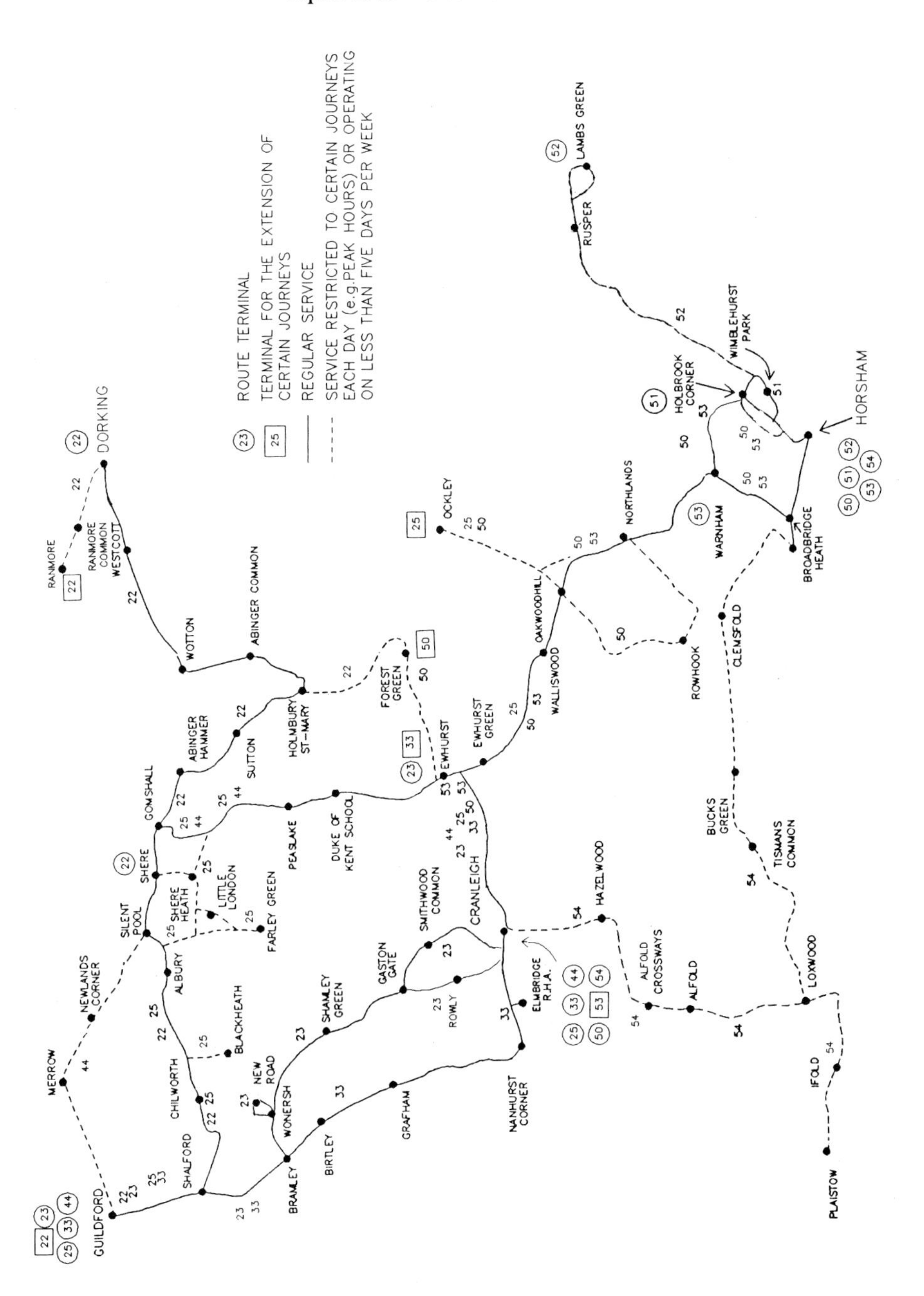

## Tillingbourne Surrey & Sussex Services

From October 198[illegible]

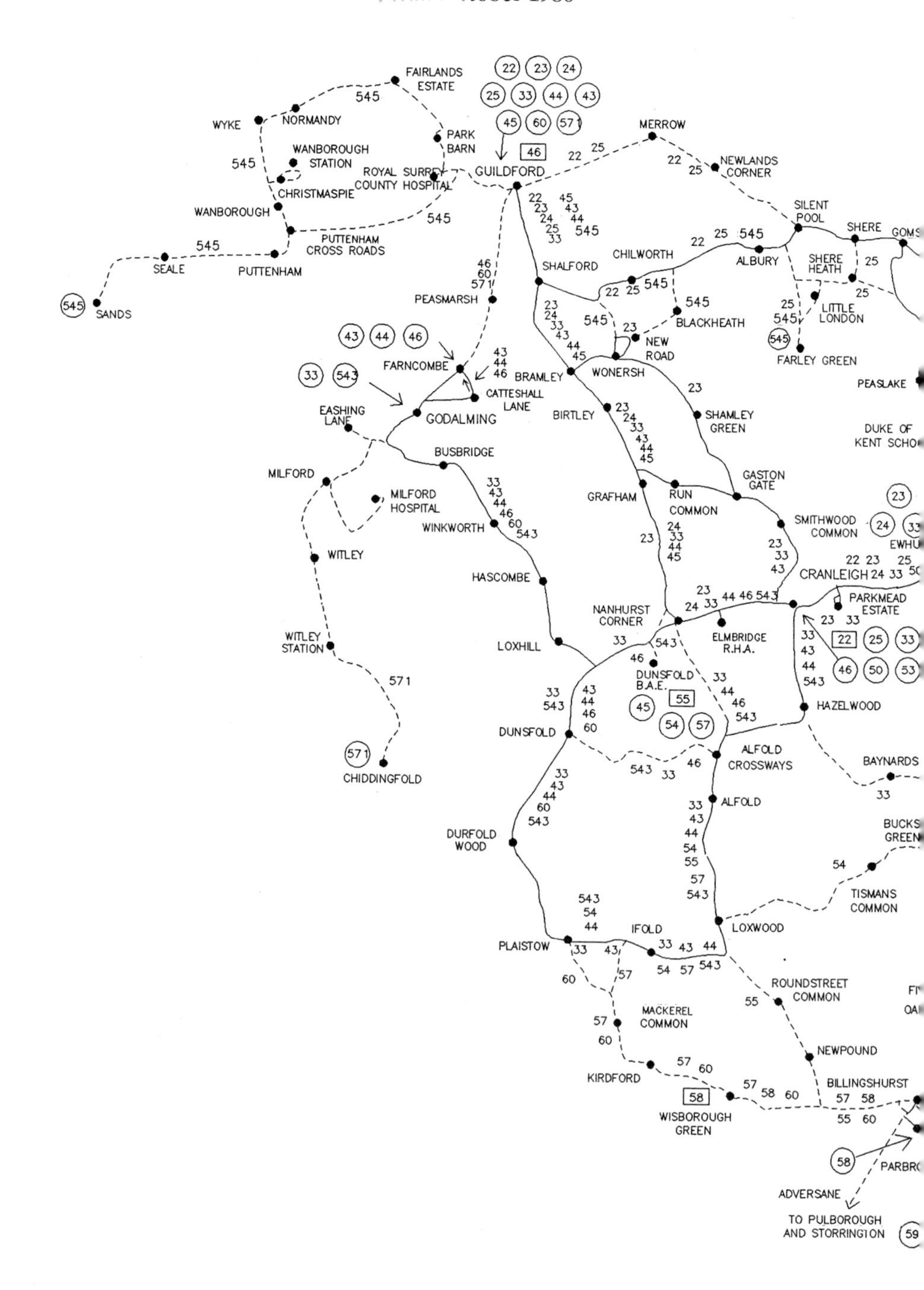

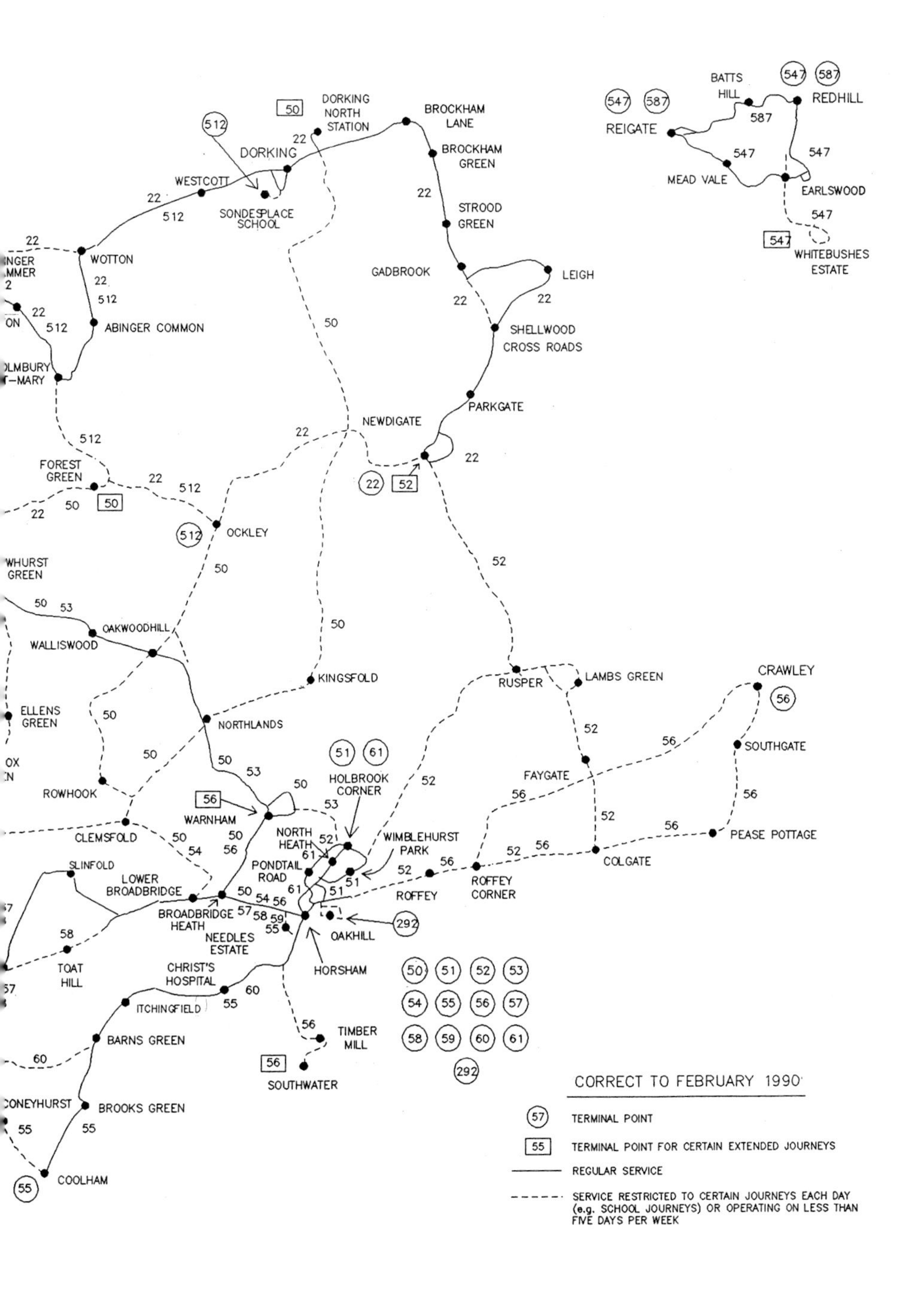
DORKING NORTH STATION
BROCKHAM LANE
BROCKHAM GREEN
DORKING
WESTCOTT
SONDES PLACE SCHOOL
STROOD GREEN
REIGATE
BATTS HILL
REDHILL
MEAD VALE
EARLSWOOD
WHITEBUSHES ESTATE
WOTTON
ABINGER COMMON
GADBROOK
LEIGH
SHELLWOOD CROSS ROADS
PARKGATE
NEWDIGATE
FOREST GREEN
OCKLEY
OAKWOODHILL
WALLISWOOD
KINGSFOLD
RUSPER
LAMBS GREEN
CRAWLEY
SOUTHGATE
ELLENS GREEN
NORTHLANDS
FAYGATE
ROWHOOK
HOLBROOK CORNER
WARNHAM
CLEMSFOLD
NORTH HEATH
WIMBLEHURST PARK
PEASE POTTAGE
COLGATE
SLINFOLD
PONDTAIL ROAD
LOWER BROADBRIDGE
ROFFEY
ROFFEY CORNER
BROADBRIDGE HEATH
NEEDLES ESTATE
OAKHILL
TOAT HILL
HORSHAM
CHRIST'S HOSPITAL
ITCHINGFIELD
TIMBER MILL
BARNS GREEN
SOUTHWATER
BROOKS GREEN
COOLHAM
CORRECT TO FEBRUARY 1990
TERMINAL POINT
TERMINAL POINT FOR CERTAIN EXTENDED JOURNEYS
REGULAR SERVICE
SERVICE RESTRICTED TO CERTAIN JOURNEYS EACH DAY (e.g. SCHOOL JOURNEYS) OR OPERATING ON LESS THAN FIVE DAYS PER WEEK

1. Tillingbourne's founder George Trice is seen here in later life together with assorted livestock. (D.Trice Collection)

2. George Trice Junior acquired control of the bus side of the business on the death of his father in 1933.
(D.Trice Collection)

# CHAPTER 1 - THE FORMATIVE YEARS

Although the precise origins of the Company are uncertain, one account of Tilling- bourne's inception concerns Mr J Vic Smith of Chilworth, who ran a cycle shop. A route through the Tillingbourne Valley had been operated since 1914 by the Aldershot and District Traction Company, except for a break between December 1916 and September 1919 caused by the First World War. Originally operated between Guildford and Leatherhead via Shalford, Chilworth, Albury, Shere, Gomshall, Abinger Hammer, Westcott, Dorking and Mickleham, after the War the route ran between Guildford and Dorking (White Horse) only, with four return journeys per day until August 1920. Thereafter the route, which was by now numbered 25, was extended to Dorking (LBSC) Station and increased to six return journeys per day. In June 1922, Aldershot and District extended two journeys on route 25 to Aldershot via Normandy and Ash, and the following year the route was sufficiently successful to be increased to an hourly frequency with all journeys being extended to Aldershot. There were also additional short workings between Shere and Guildford which were numbered 26.

**3. This 14 seater Chevrolet is believed to have been Tillingbourne's first vehicle in 1924. (A.Lambert Collection)**

Apparently, one day early in 1924 Mr Smith missed the bus from Gomshall to Guildford and, rather than wait for the next one, he walked to town whilst conjecturing over the possibilities of starting an additional bus service between those places. He canvassed the support of several local people, including his father and an uncle. Trice seems to have become involved at this stage, although who approached who is unclear. In any case, the two men became partners.

**4. PE 1279 was an Overland 14 seater, possibly purchased when the Albury route commenced. (A.Lambert Collection)**

A fourteen seater was purchased and it entered service between Gomshall and Guildford, via Shere, Newlands Corner and Merrow, on Easter Bank Holiday, 1924, on an hourly frequency with a through fare of 1/- single, the vehicle being kept near Mr Smith's cycle shop. The start date of the service is also quoted as Derby Day, 1924. Soon after, a second route to Guildford was introduced, starting at Albury. Trice and Smith continued in partnership until the late 1920s, when Trice became the sole proprietor, although Smith's involvement in the business appears to have been limited.

Fourteen seater Overland and Chevrolet vehicles, painted maroon and bearing the fleetname "Tillingbourne Valley", were used on the bus routes: Guildford to Gomshall Station via Merrow, Newlands Corner and Shere and Guildford to Albury Park Gates via Shalford, Chilworth and Albury Village.

The village of Ewhurst, some miles to the south of Gomshall, was the base for George Readings' Surrey Hills Motor Services business, and in the early 1920s he had operated Ford Model Ts between Cranleigh and Gomshall Station (connecting with the trains) via Ewhurst, Peaslake and Shere. A timetable dating from October 1924 shows a thrice weekly service from Holmbury St.Mary to Guildford running via the A & D 25 route from Abinger Hammer, although there is some doubt as to whether this actually operated. Delivery of five Lancia buses preceded the introduction in June 1925 of a route from Ewhurst/Holmbury St.Mary to Peaslake, Gomshall, Shere, Newlands Corner, Merrow and Guildford, thus paralleling one of Trice and Smith's routes. By now, Tillingbourne had extended the Gomshall service to Peaslake.

**5. One of the secondhand vehicles purchased to replace those lost in the depot fire in 1928 was YB 9506, an 18 seat Dennis G. Note the contemporary cinema posters. (P.Lacey Collection)**

However, Surrey Hills' expansion had also caused concern to both Aldershot and District and to the Reigate based East Surrey Traction Company, although amicable arrangements had been made in the Dorking area between Surrey Hills and East Surrey. Accordingly, East Surrey's backers, London General Omnibus Company, contributed financially towards A & D's acquisition of Surrey Hills on 10 January 1926, together with the Ewhurst garage and the Lancia vehicles. This garage subsequently passed through several hands and, coincidentally was to play a major role in the affairs of the Tillingbourne Company in the 1970s. With the aid of the purchase money, Readings moved to Cheltenham and founded the famous long-distance coaching firm Black and White Motorways. A & D operated the

Guildford via Newlands Corner route under the Surrey Hills title until 14 July 1926 when it was withdrawn.

Although the purchase of Surrey Hills removed an energetic competitor from the scene, it did little to resolve the boundary dispute between East Surrey and A & D over running rights on the Dorking to Guildford road. Thus the three companies commenced negotiations over these matters in the summer following the Surrey Hills take over, but they were not concluded until 27 September 1927. The terms allowed for equal operation by both A & D and East Surrey on several existing and proposed routes, including the 25 between Guildford and Dorking

**6. Magnet Omnibus Service was in competition with Tillingbourne between Guildford and Peaslake after July 1926. PH 6509, seen here at the Hurtwood Inn Peaslake, was a Chevrolet LM which was sold with the service to London Transport in March 1934. (B.LeJeune Collection)**

(previously an A & D monopoly) and Ewhurst and Guildford via Peaslake, Gomshall, Shere, Newlands Corner and Merrow. However, going back to 1926, as East Surrey at that time lacked vehicles to participate in the latter service, they objected strongly to A & D's continued operation of the former Surrey Hills service via Newlands Corner, and this was the reason for its withdrawal. Instead, A & D extended its existing 25B service, which ran from Guildford to Peaslake via Shalford, Chilworth, Albury, Shere and Gomshall to Ewhurst and increased the frequency.

The disappearance of the Surrey Hills route must have come as a temporary relief to the Tillingbourne concern, although it seems to have encouraged another new operator, A R Rudall of Guildford, trading as Magnet Omnibus Service, to start a service at this time from Guildford to Peaslake via Newlands Corner.

Trice and Smith expanded their operations through Chilworth probably in 1926 when the Guildford to Albury Park Gates route was extended to Brook and Farley Green, and on Tuesdays, Fridays and Saturdays certain extra journeys diverged at Chilworth Station to ascend to Blackheath, a small hamlet containing a few houses, Haywards Garage and little else.

Despite the conclusion of the agreement between East Surrey, A & D and London General in September 1927, the transfer of two of the former Surrey Hills

**7. New in 1929 was PK 5889, a Dennis G here labelled for the short-lived Dorking service, which competed with East Surrey and Aldershot & District. (T.Brown Collection)**

Lancia buses to East Surrey and the long standing desire of the East Surrey Company to participate in the 25 route between Dorking and Guildford, a continued shortage of vehicles prevented immediate action. During the protracted negotiations the LGOC had confided to East Surrey that, if the discussions should not be successful, East Surrey should operate some of the routes in direct competition with A & D, and it is interesting to speculate how history may have

**8. Looking very smart in their white dustcoats are drivers Joe Vincent and Bert Woolgar, posing by Thornycroft A2 PG 8268. (T.Brown Collection)**

been changed had open warfare broken out between the two companies. However by early 1928 the LGOC had managed to find four surplus single deck K type buses to transfer to East Surrey, and on 29 February of that year East Surrey began operating route 25 between Dorking and Guildford which resulted in a basic joint half hourly headway with A & D. Also on that day a new service, route 44, commenced joint operation on an hourly basis between Guildford and Peaslake via Newlands Corner with certain A & D journeys continuing through to Ewhurst. A & D continued to use the former Surrey Hills garage to house the vehicle operating this service, however East Surrey had to supply their vehicle from as far away as Leatherhead garage. As a result of these changes, A & D withdrew their 25B service.

A.T.Brady of Forest Green (Brown Motor Services, but originally trading as Forest Green and District Omnibus Service) had been running from Gomshall Station to Horsham via Forest Green since about 1924, and in February 1928 the northern part of the route was incorporated into a two hourly service from Forest Green to Guildford via Holmbury St.Mary, Abinger Hammer, Gomshall, Shere,

Albury, Chilworth and Shalford, thus providing yet more competition for the Tillingbourne service along the valley road.

The Tillingbourne concern suffered a cruel blow on Saturday, 10 March 1928 when a serious fire destroyed the original garage at 97 New Road Chilworth, together with three 14 seater vehicles, as well as damaging another which had recently been delivered, and causing an estimated £2,000 worth of damage. The last bus back from Guildford had been garaged the previous night by driver G.Worsfold, who noticed nothing amiss. At 4 am, Mr Poulter who lived next door discovered the fire and woke Mr Trice, who found the corrugated iron roof had become red hot, and was thwarted by the intense heat and dense smoke while trying to save the buses. It was a very cold frosty morning and it is recalled that when the firemen arrived, some promptly fell over on the ice which covered the road. The blaze was under control in two hours, but the origin of the fire remained a mystery. Naturally the conflagration caused considerable local excitement, but it appears that the occupant of the house two doors away slept through it all! In order to keep

**9. The 18 seat body by Short Bros. on Thornycroft A2 PG 8268 offered new standards of comfort when delivered in 1930. (P.Lacey Collection)**

services running, Trice had to borrow vehicles from other local companies, including Yellow Bus Services of Stoughton.

After acquiring some replacement vehicles for those lost in the fire, the Blackheath journeys were discontinued in about 1929, and the service to Guildford from Farley Green and Albury was operated to an hourly frequency each day of the week. In August of that year, Trice turned his thoughts to expansion and commenced a daily service to Dorking along the A & D/East Surrey route 25 from Gomshall, Abinger Hammer and Westcott. This new competition was regarded with distaste by the established operators who employed the usual measures when dealing with a small operator of this nature which challenged their supremacy. They ran "chaser" duplicates on service 25 and Tillingbourne revenue suffered accordingly. On one occasion three consecutive journeys carried no passengers at all, and an extension from Gomshall to Peaslake did little to improve matters. Trice probably initiated the Dorking service in retaliation for "chasers" being run by the large companies in front of his vehicles between Albury and Guildford. No improvement in revenue brought about the abandonment of the service in

**10. Photographed before delivery in 1931 was Dennis GL, PL 5339. The 20 seat body was also by Dennis. (P.Lacey Collection)**

November 1929, at which time all the offending "chasers" were withdrawn by agreement with A & D and East Surrey.

Back in November 1926, the Guildford Town Council Watch Committee had approved an application by Yellow Bus Services of Stoughton to operate a service from the Town Centre to Tyting Hill, via Onslow Street, Upper High Street, Warren Road and One Tree Corner. Yellow Bus had wished to operate a service to the Merrow area for some time, however this route was to be their only foray into the eastern side of town, and it has been said that their old Chevrolet buses often had difficulty making the climb up Warren Road, particularly during wintertime in the ice and snow. Yellow Buses decided to withdraw the service in 1929, and operation was transferred to Tillingbourne in December of that year, being worked by vehicles employed on the Farley Green service during layover time, to an hourly frequency, similar to that provided by Yellow Bus.

Competition along the valley road continued to be intense and from 24 February 1930, A & D, East Surrey, Tillingbourne and A T Brady introduced a co-ordinated timetable between Guildford and Albury. This was followed on 1 December by an agreement between the former three concerns and also Magnet for a co-ordinated timetable between Guildford and Peaslake via Newlands Corner.

In April 1930, Aldershot and District made a written plea to the Guildford Watch Committee that, when applications for licence renewals in respect of the Newlands Corner route were considered, only the existing operators should be favoured. Local Guildford operator Safeguard requested permission to run journeys between the Town and Newlands Corner on Sundays and Public Holidays, but this was

**11. PJ 717 was a Bedford WLB with 20 seat Duple coachwork and was believed to be the first vehicle in Lionel Rhees's Tillingbourne Valley Coaches fleet in October 1931, being used on Excursions and Private Hire. (P.Lacey Collection)**

refused by the Watch Committee, which body appeared to be adopting a stance of encouraging co-ordination between various operators on common sections of route.

On 7 October 1931 a limited company, Tillingbourne Valley Bus Services Ltd. was incorporated with a capital of £2500 in £1 shares, the directors being George and Margaret Trice and Harry Ebben. The latter was in a clerical position at a garage in Godalming and held a nominal one share, having no involvement in the running of the Tillingbourne business.

The Road Traffic Act 1930 came into effect during 1931 and took service and vehicle licensing out of the hands of the local councils and placed them under the control of an area Traffic Commissioner. Until that time, licensing for bus routes,

**12. Seen on the Farley Green service is DPC 200, new in 1935 and purchased direct from the Thornycroft stand at the Motor Show at Olympia. It was a "Handy" model with 20 seat body by Waveney. (T.Brown Collection)**

drivers, conductors and vehicles had been a task for the Guildford Town Watch Committee. Unfortunately, the Committee minutes for the period up to December 1929 are untraceable, and had they been available, the dating of Tillingbourne's activities during the formative years would have been more accurate. Under the new scenario, Guildford and Tillingbourne's operating territory were placed in the Metropolitan Traffic Area. As Tillingbourne's operations were well established, the company was granted licenses for its three bus services, as well as for excursions picking up at Chilworth. Albury, Farley Green etc.

On 20 January 1932, East Surrey became part of London General Country Services Ltd. (a subsidiary of its parent, London General Omnibus Co.), set up to encompass East Surrey and the operations of the National Omnibus and Transport Co. Ltd. to the north of London. This had no immediate effect on bus services in the Tilling- bourne area.

Tillingbourne Valley was granted a short period license for a special service to Albury Flower Show on 13 July 1932, quite a major local event at that time, and this was repeated for several subsequent years.

**13. This Thornycroft "Dainty", GPB 957, also had a body by Waveney and was photographed at One Tree Corner on the Warren Road route. (T.Brown Collection)**

**14. Thornycroft "Nippy" HPL 265 is seen in Guildford during the last War. The poster behind it reminds us that Diptheria was still a serious threat to health in those days. (J.Parke)**

In 1933 George Trice died and the business passed to his son, also George, and to his son-in-law, Lionel Rhees. The latter, who lived at 107 New Road, had already become involved by this time, as the July 1931 Tillingbourne Valley excursion licence was in his name. A new 20 seat Bedford WLB, first licenced in October 1931, is thought to have been owned by him, rather than Trice, but it carried Tillingbourne Valley livery and fleetname. Now, by mutual agreement, Trice continued to run the bus services whilst Rhees traded separately as Tillingbourne Valley Coaches. The latter continued the private hire and excursion work. Rhees did not inherit any vehicles with his part of the business, but ran two or three small coaches, usually of Bedford or Commer manufacture, in a similar livery to that of the buses, but with the addition of cream rather than grey. He used a garage situated adjacent to Trice's second premises in New Road, opposite the original Tillingbourne garage at No. 97.

The all-embracing London Passenger Transport Board (London Transport) had been set up under an Act of Parliament and from 1 July 1933 the Country Bus Department of London Transport, based at Reigate, took over the London General Country Services and also the Aldershot and District workings on service 25 a month later, renumbering it 425 from the same date but running between Dorking and Guildford only. From 3 August, service 44 was renumbered 448 and LT acquired the A & D share of the timings, together with certain vehicles and the bus garage at Ewhurst.

Tillingbourne's bus services had not been included on the list of those to be acquired under LPTB's compulsory purchase powers, but the Board was able to acquire services wholly or partly in its operating area, especially where there was an element of competition. Trice was prepared to sell his share of the Guildford-Peaslake journeys but wished to retain his other two services. London Transport desired to acquire all three, so began to pressure Tillingbourne by not granting consent for the carriage of local passengers in the Board's "Special Area", including the lucrative Guildford - Merrow section. Passenger inconvenience that resulted sparked an angry public reaction and LT was forced to grant consent on a temporary basis. A substantial petition was submitted to the Guildford Watch Committee in January 1934 from persons disadvantaged by the restrictions, and the matter was pursued with the LPTB.

During 1933, a proposal was put before the Town Watch Committee to use the section of Guildford Cattle Market nearest to Woodbridge Road as a bus station in order to relieve the congested street parking arrangements. However, it was not until after the Second World War that new bus stations were finally constructed, as will be mentioned later.

In December 1933, Tillingbourne applied to the Traffic Commissioner for a new service from Farley Green to Guildford via Park Gates, Albury, Blackheath and Shalford, but the application was refused the following month.

London Transport acquired the journeys operated by Magnet between Guildford and Peaslake on 7 March 1934, together with two 14 seat Chevrolet vehicles, giving it an overall two-thirds share in the service. This was followed by an offer from LT to purchase Trice's business voluntarily, but this offer was declined. The consent to carry passengers in the "Special Area" was renewed annually until 1969, when the Transport (London) Act removed such a requirement.

**15. Another wartime view: Awaiting departure for Farley Green is JPK 518, a Dodge RBF with Harrington bodywork. It originated in the Isle of Man and was purchased by Trice through a dealer, only lasting a short time in the fleet. Note the masked headlamps. (J.Parke)**

**16. Tillingbourne received one of the ubiquitous wartime utility Bedford OWB's with Duple bodywork featuring wooden slatted seats. JPL 88 is on the Peaslake service and is breasting the North Downs at Newlands Corner. (T.Brown Collection)**

The timetables for the Peaslake and Farley Green services were further co-ordinated with London Transport from 24 April 1935 and an agreement was made regarding reciprocal arrangements for the acceptance of each others return tickets. On 30 April 1935 Tillingbourne Valley Bus Services Ltd. was retitled Tillingbourne Valley Services Ltd., and the bus routes continued virtually unaltered until well after the Second World War. After the depot fire, Tillingbourne's fleet consisted of Dennis G and Thornycroft A2 vehicles, and these were replaced from November 1934 onwards by several 20 seater Thornycrofts of the Handy, Nippy and Dainty models.

The war years presented Tillingbourne with staffing and vehicle maintenance problems whilst restrictions on private motoring put pressure on available bus service capacity. A second-hand 20 seater Dodge was owned for a brief period between 1942 and 1943 and January 1943 saw the delivery of one of the ubiquitous Bedford OWB utility 32 seat buses, built to a government standard austere specification and only delivered to operators who could demonstrate real need for additional vehicles. As the Tillingbourne routes were only licenced for vehicles with a 20 seat maximum capacity, twelve seats had to be removed!

Apart from the withdrawal of certain late evening cinema buses, the time- tables during the War were largely unchanged. Military personnel were billeted in some of the larger houses in the area whilst there was a huge ammunition dump at Shere. Prior to D-Day in 1944, men and vehicles were held ready under the trees on Albury Heath. The A25 road, which in those days was quite narrow, was an important traffic artery and frequently Tillingbourne buses were delayed by convoys of heavy vehicles. These included some dummy tanks made out of cardboard and mounted over lorries which were designed to fool any Luftwaffe surveillance aircraft. This road was so important that field telephones and fire extinguishers were located at frequent intervals along its length. During the War, George Trice and his son, Derek, were responsible for the formation of the volunteer Chilworth Fire Brigade, and the two appliances were kept in the second Tillingbourne garage. The local brigade continued in existence for over twenty years.

During 1940 work was progressing on construction work at Dunsfold Aerodrome, near Cranleigh. Vehicles from Rhees' Tillingbourne Valley Coaches fleet were amongst those employed for transporting the workforce, and at the weekends a Rhees vehicle could sometimes be hired to Yellow Bus which was short of vehicles at that time. When the latter's situation subsequently improved it would loan a vehicle to Rhees to enable maintenance to proceed on his vehicles. As the work at Dunsfold was of national importance, Rhees was able to obtain two utility Bedford OWB s, similar to the one owned by Trice.

# CHAPTER 2 - TRIALS AND TRIBULATIONS

The first new postwar vehicle was delivered in February 1946, being another 20 seater Thornycroft Nippy and a not altogether popular vehicle. This proved to be the last new vehicle acquired by the Company whilst it remained in the hands of the Trice family. In September of that year, Trice again tried to serve Blackheath by applying for a service between Chilworth Station and Guildford via Blackheath, Barnett Hill and Shalford. This proposal attracted objections from London Transport and A & D, so the application was withdrawn in November to avoid any conflict with Tillingbourne's powerful neighbours. However, this cautious attitude did not deter Lionel Rhees of Tillingbourne Valley Coaches from applying in October 1947 for a Blackheath-Barnett Hill-Guildford service, and this was granted as a limited stop facility operating on Tuesdays, Thursdays, Fridays and Saturdays with one round trip on which only return fares to Guildford were available. An application was made in August 1950 to divert the route to pick up at Chilworth and Shalford, but this was not proceeded with, probably due to objections.

**17. The last new vehicle of the Trice era was also the first postwar delivery. KPE 425 was a Thornycroft Nippy with Thurgood 20 seat bodywork and was not exactly popular at Chilworth. This Thornycroft publicity photograph was posed in Shere and is very evocative of the period. (D.Trice Collection)**

After the War, a development of chalet-type accommodation known as "Treetops Holiday Camp" was established in Shophouse Lane, some distance beyond the terminus of the Farley Green service, and certain journeys on that route were extended to Treetops during the summer months when required. The road is rather narrow and tortuous and must have caused some difficulties even for the small vehicles used by Tillingbourne at that time. However, by the time that the Farley Green service was regularly extended to terminate at Kingsfield in February 1956, the Treetops journeys had ceased. The holiday chalets remain to this day and present a scene probably little changed since the halcyon days of the British Holiday in the early post-war era.

**18. Later in its life the side of KPE 425 was decorated with a "scroll"- type fleetname in place of the original "garter" device. It is seen here on the Warren Road route in the 1950's. (N.Hamshere)**

On 1 December 1948, Harry Ebben's share in Tillingbourne Valley Services Ltd was acquired by George Trice, who had retired from day to day involvement in the Company and his son Derek had become manager in 1948. About this time a purchase offer for the business was received from Basil Williams of Emsworth, whose Hants and Sussex Motor Services group of companies operated several rural bus services over a wide area of Hampshire and West Sussex. Since the War, Hants and Sussex had expanded by piecemeal acquisition of small operators, and one of its subsidiaries, F.H.Kilner (Transport) Ltd., had a route which entered Surrey, being the Ewhurst to Horsham, via Walliswood, Oakwoodhill and Rowhook service taken over from A.Lazzell in 1946. Williams had attempted in 1949 to get a better foothold in Surrey by trying to purchase the Guildford to Camberley service of Yellow Bus, a route that had been offered for sale. Sydney Hayter of Yellow Bus wanted more for the route than Williams was prepared to pay, and the latter's attempt to acquire Tillingbourne was not taken seriously by the Trice family. London Transport had been troubled by Williams' expansion plans in the Horsham area, and to ensure this was not repeated, they also put in an offer for Tillingbourne, which was also refused by Trice.

Following the death of Lionel Rhees, an application was made in May 1953 to transfer the licences of Tillingbourne Valley Coaches to his second wife Hilda. A year later this business was sold to H.D.Rackcliffe of Guildford, who reduced the Blackheath bus service to operate on Fridays only. In February 1955, Rackcliffe sold out to Cookes Coaches (Stoughton) Ltd., who soon withdrew the Blackheath service. Another operator was involved in the local coaching market as, at the end of 1954, Montague Tullett of Shere, trading as Shere Coaches, had applied for excursions from Peaslake, Gomshall and Shere.

**19. As revenue income dropped, new vehicles could not be justified. Instead, a number of secondhand purchases entered the fleet from 1950 onwards. The first was JXH 720, a Pearson-bodied Bedford OB. (N.Hamshere)**

Derek Trice had other business interests and he now found himself rather reluctantly in charge of a bus company, whose rural services showed little promise of high revenue yield and whose fleet was somewhat run-down after the shortages and rigours of wartime operation.

During the 1950s there was a complete change-over in the Tillingbourne fleet, with a steady influx of Bedford OBs together with three similar Austin CX buses,

20. Another unusual body was that by Woodall Nicholson on Bedford OB MNU 689 which was purchased from Booth & Fisher of Halfway, Yorks. It is seen at Stand 14 in the Farnham Road Bus Station in Guildford, used by the Farley Green and Warren Road services and also by Brown Motor Services for their Forest Green route. (N.Hamshere)

21. Also carrying Pearson bodywork was NGX 513, an Austin CXB which was previously a lorry with Manchester Co-op and was subsequently rebodied as a coach. At Farnham Road Bus Station on 9 October 1955. (J.Gillham)

**22. On the same day, the other Austin in the fleet, EKU 810 with a Plaxton body, was on the Peaslake service at the Onslow Street Bus Station. (J.Gillham)**

**23. JTB 262 was the second Bedford OB with unusual full-front Plaxton bodywork to be purchased. (D.Stuttard)**

replacing time-expired vehicles. These acquisitions were all secondhand, whereas from 1929 to 1946 virtually all vehicles had been purchased new, an indication that the revenue from the bus routes was no longer sufficient to justify investment in new rolling stock. A 35 seater Bedford SBG with Burlingham Seagull coach body acquired in July 1960 for private hire work was to be the largest capacity vehicle operated by the Trice family. From 1953, London Transport had taken delivery of eighty four 26 seater single deckers known as the GS class, being one man operated and ideal for use on sparsely-trafficked rural routes in their country area. The chassis was the normal control Guy Special NVLLP which was based on the Vixen model and the bodywork was by Eastern Coachworks (ECW) of Lowestoft, displaying some of their contemporary design features although still having a strong family resemblance to the standard LT single decker of that period, the RF class. However, with the withdrawal of several rural routes operated by these GS vehicles and with the availability of the larger RF buses newly converted for driver-only operation, the need for GS vehicles had greatly diminished. A number were therefore surplus to LT's requirements and they began to be sold off in the early 1960s.

**24. An example of the standard Bedford OB/Duple Vista combination is OEV 889, previously used as Works transport by Lancing & Bagnall at Basingstoke. This view dates from the early 1960's. (G.Burgess)**

At this time, the general condition of both bodywork and mechanical side of the Tillingbourne fleet was a cause of considerable concern to Trice, who was actively looking for suitable replacement vehicles without any success. The availability of these relatively young vehicles was a godsend to the Company, and in 1963 the "GS era" in the Tillingbourne Valley fleet began with the purchase of five of the type to

**25. TMY 26 seems to have sustained some accident damage to the off-side front wing! Also visible at Farnham Road Bus Stn. are an Aldershot & District Dennis Lance double decker and a Thames Valley Bristol LS on the joint TV/A&D service 75 to Reading. (Authors Collection)**

**26. With 35 seats, this was the largest vehicle owned by the Trice family. GHS 721 was a Bedford SBG with attractive Burlingham body and was purchased in July 1960 with thoughts of Private Hire revenue. (D.Trice Collection)**

replace the entire existing fleet. They were the first diesel engined buses to be operated by Tillingbourne Valley, and in Price's view were the perfect vehicle for rural services, not only in terms of fuel consumption, but also because of their low maintenance costs and overall reliability.

**27. Between March 1963 and August 1964 both London Transport and Tillingbourne operated Guy GS-type vehicles between Guildford and Peaslake. The former's green-liveried GS 66 loads at Onslow Street Bus Station for a service 448 journey to Ewhurst. (Authors Collection)**

Interestingly, Tillingbourne Valley had never used route numbers for their services, and even the joint operation of route 448 did not result in that number being displayed on Tillingbourne buses. The livery had remained a dark maroon, with light grey relief, on pre-war vehicles the fleet name was displayed on the sides prominently in a "script" style, this later being replaced by a "scroll" containing the Company's name while the one post war new vehicle had a "garter" device. The later Bedfords, Austins and the GSs had no fleetname displayed, however the GSs did have fleet numbers which were in gold lettering with a circle around them. Thus from 1963 both maroon liveried and dark green LT GSs could be seen jointly operating the 448 service, the latter replacing pre-war Leyland Cub vehicles in the nineteen fifties. By 1963, London Transport route 425 was being operated with RF class vehicles, which featured a Metro Cammell body on an AEC Regal IV chassis.

In 1964, Tillingbourne Valley purchased a further three GSs to assist with an expansion in operations. Declining traffic had caused London Transport to review its operations on route 448, and it concluded that it was no longer economic to continue them. LT approached Tillingbourne to see if it would be interested in running the whole service, including the Ewhurst journeys, and also offered to hand over local Guildford service 448A from the town centre to Pewley Way which dated from August 1950 and was worked by buses from route 448 during layover time. Instead of actually selling these services to Tillingbourne, it was proposed that Tillingbourne should pay 5% of the additional gross receipts to LT, up to a maximum of £550 per annum. After considering the proposal, Tillingbourne accepted and commenced sole operation of services 448 and 448A from 12 August 1964.

However, the mid nineteen sixties were not halcyon days for rural bus services and, within a year, Trice was forced to take a critical look at his expanded operations. Ridership and revenue were declining and there were three staff vacancies in a total requirement of nine drivers. In reality, no money was ever paid to London Transport. The additional revenue obtained by Tillingbourne was so poor that when the first payment was due, Trice claimed the amount was unreasonable and that, if LT felt compelled to press for payment, he would be forced to hand back the journeys to them. Trice's plea was recognised as Tillingbourne was officially released from the "commission" payments as there were not likely to be any additional receipts in which LT could claim a share.

**28. Although London Transport no longer ran to Peaslake after 11 August 1964, a few of their concrete bus stop poles remained in place, some of them later carrying ex-Aldershot & District flags erected by Tillingbourne. (J.Gaff)**

Immediate action was required and service reductions were effected from 28 November 1965 involving all routes. The frequency of the Peaslake service was reduced from every 30 minutes to every 45 minutes, and the through journeys to Ewhurst were withdrawn, together with all Pewley Way services. The frequency of the Farley Green and Warren Road routes was halved so that they each operated two-hourly. Between Peaslake and Ewhurst there are only a few scattered dwellings, thus there is minimal intermediate traffic potential and Ewhurst itself had a more frequent and direct service to Guildford via Cranleigh, being A & D's long-standing service 23.

During this period the Tillingbourne Valley fleet was a model example of standardisation, with eight maroon liveried GSs being operated on the remaining three bus services. Some were sold or stripped for spares in the late nineteen sixties, although additional examples were purchased as replacements, one being GS82 which had been demoted to LT's service vehicle fleet as a "civil defence" vehicle. However, this standardisation was to be in complete contrast to that which was to follow in the new decade, a period which was to bring mixed fortunes to the bus industry and cause many significant events to happen in the Tillingbourne Valley.

Under the Transport Act (London) of 1969, the Country Bus and Greenline operations of London Transport were hived off from 1 January 1970 to a new concern, London Country Bus Services Ltd., a subsidiary of the National Bus Company based at the old East Surrey headquarters in Reigate. Initially there was little outward change visible to operations of service 425. Tom Brady, the proprietor of Brown Motor Services retired on 31 October 1970 and his business passed to North Downs Rural Transport Ltd., a company headed by John Wylde of Orpington. The Forest Green to Guildford via Holmbury St.Mary, Abinger Hammer, Gomshall, Shere, Albury, Chilworth and Shalford service was numbered 845 by North Downs and early the following year Brady's usual vehicles on the service, a Marshall bodied Bedford VAS1 and a Willowbrook bodied Albion Nimbus were supplemented by two further Nimbus vehicles acquired from Western Welsh, and painted in the erstwhile Brady livery of brown and cream.

**29. Tillingbourne purchased their first three GS's from London Transport for £600 each in March 1963, including GS 3 and they were soon re-painted into the new owner's maroon livery. (Authors Collection)**

**30. MXX 325 arrived in October 1964 and fleet numbers were applied to the all-GS fleet at that time. GS 25 often worked on route 448 during its LT days and it was back on its old stamping ground in this December 1964 view. Note how the route number has been painted out on the ex-LT blind. (J.Gaff)**

**31. Although purchased in May 1964, MXX 376 did not enter service until 12 August when Tillingbourne took over LT route 448A from Guildford to Pewley Way (redesignated Pewley Hill on this blind), and it was photographed two days later. (J.Gaff)**

After the Second World War, Derek Trice had opened the garage at 97 New Road for general motor repairs, the buses being concentrated at the garage on the north side of the road in the 1950s. He also ran a solid fuel-to-oil boiler conversion business from showrooms in Guildford and subsequently developed a domestic fuel-oil distribution business at New Road known as Oilheat Services (Guildford) Ltd. Expansion of these activities paralleled a decline in the bus services. Formerly, the buses were expected to return an operating profit, but by the 1960s they relied on a degree of cross-subsidisation from the garage business in terms of vehicle maintenance and general overheads, possibly disguising the true cost of running them. Furthermore, the Trice family felt an obligation towards their employees, many of whom had been with the Company since the pre-war era. Against this background, the Trice family made a decision to sell the company. George Trice had recently died, and his widow and son felt that now was an appropriate time to dispose of the bus business.

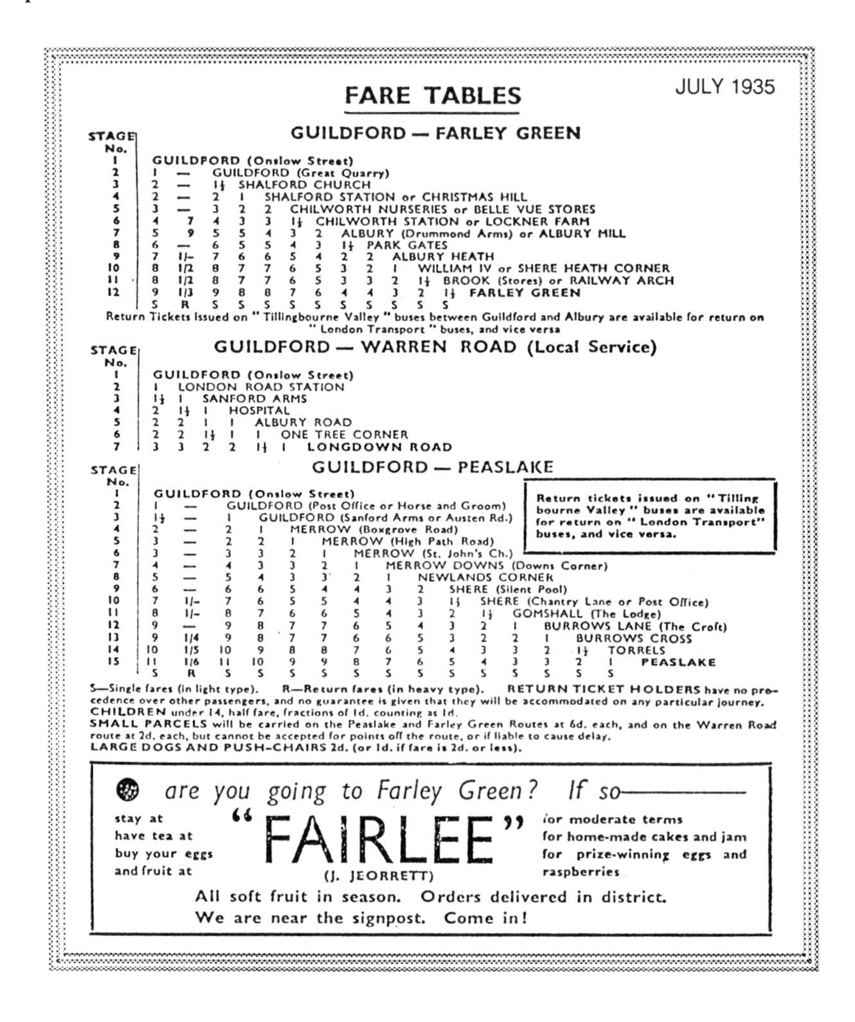

## FARE TABLES

JULY 1935

### GUILDFORD — FARLEY GREEN

| STAGE No. | | | | | | | | | | | | | |
|---|---|---|---|---|---|---|---|---|---|---|---|---|---|
| 1 | GUILDFORD (Onslow Street) | | | | | | | | | | | | |
| 2 | 1 | — | GUILDFORD (Great Quarry) | | | | | | | | | | |
| 3 | 2 | — | 1½ | SHALFORD CHURCH | | | | | | | | | |
| 4 | 2 | — | 2 | 1 | SHALFORD STATION or CHRISTMAS HILL | | | | | | | | |
| 5 | 3 | — | 3 | 2 | 2 | CHILWORTH NURSERIES or BELLE VUE STORES | | | | | | | |
| 6 | 4 | 7 | 4 | 3 | 3 | 1½ | CHILWORTH STATION or LOCKNER FARM | | | | | | |
| 7 | 5 | 9 | 5 | 5 | 4 | 3 | 2 | ALBURY (Drummond Arms) or ALBURY MILL | | | | | |
| 8 | 6 | — | 6 | 5 | 5 | 4 | 3 | 1½ | PARK GATES | | | | |
| 9 | 7 | 1/- | 7 | 6 | 6 | 5 | 4 | 2 | 2 | ALBURY HEATH | | | |
| 10 | 8 | 1/2 | 8 | 7 | 7 | 6 | 5 | 3 | 2 | 1 | WILLIAM IV or SHERE HEATH CORNER | | |
| 11 | 8 | 1/2 | 8 | 7 | 7 | 6 | 5 | 3 | 3 | 2 | 1½ | BROOK (Stores) or RAILWAY ARCH | |
| 12 | 9 | 1/3 | 9 | 8 | 8 | 7 | 6 | 4 | 4 | 3 | 2 | 1½ | FARLEY GREEN |
| | S | R | S | S | S | S | S | S | S | S | S | S | |

Return Tickets issued on "Tillingbourne Valley" buses between Guildford and Albury are available for return on "London Transport" buses, and vice versa

### GUILDFORD — WARREN ROAD (Local Service)

| STAGE No. | | | | | | | |
|---|---|---|---|---|---|---|---|
| 1 | GUILDFORD (Onslow Street) | | | | | | |
| 2 | 1 | LONDON ROAD STATION | | | | | |
| 3 | 1½ | 1 | SANFORD ARMS | | | | |
| 4 | 2 | 1½ | 1 | HOSPITAL | | | |
| 5 | 2 | 2 | 1 | 1 | ALBURY ROAD | | |
| 6 | 2 | 2 | 1½ | 1 | 1 | ONE TREE CORNER | |
| 7 | 3 | 3 | 2 | 2 | 1½ | 1 | LONGDOWN ROAD |

### GUILDFORD — PEASLAKE

| STAGE No. | | | | | | | | | | | | | | | | |
|---|---|---|---|---|---|---|---|---|---|---|---|---|---|---|---|---|
| 1 | GUILDFORD (Onslow Street) | | | | | | | | | | | | | | | |
| 2 | 1 | — | GUILDFORD (Post Office or Horse and Groom) | | | | | | | | | | | | | |
| 3 | 1½ | — | 1 | GUILDFORD (Sanford Arms or Austen Rd.) | | | | | | | | | | | | |
| 4 | 2 | — | 2 | 1 | MERROW (Boxgrove Road) | | | | | | | | | | | |
| 5 | 3 | — | 2 | 2 | 1 | MERROW (High Path Road) | | | | | | | | | | |
| 6 | 3 | — | 3 | 3 | 2 | 1 | MERROW (St. John's Ch.) | | | | | | | | | |
| 7 | 4 | — | 4 | 3 | 3 | 2 | 1 | MERROW DOWNS (Downs Corner) | | | | | | | | |
| 8 | 5 | — | 5 | 4 | 3 | 3 | 2 | 1 | NEWLANDS CORNER | | | | | | | |
| 9 | 6 | — | 6 | 6 | 5 | 4 | 4 | 3 | 2 | SHERE (Silent Pool) | | | | | | |
| 10 | 7 | 1/- | 7 | 6 | 5 | 5 | 4 | 4 | 3 | 1½ | SHERE (Chantry Lane or Post Office) | | | | | |
| 11 | 8 | 1/- | 8 | 7 | 6 | 6 | 5 | 4 | 3 | 2 | 1½ | GOMSHALL (The Lodge) | | | | |
| 12 | 9 | — | 9 | 8 | 7 | 7 | 6 | 5 | 4 | 3 | 2 | 1 | BURROWS LANE (The Croft) | | | |
| 13 | 9 | 1/4 | 9 | 8 | 7 | 7 | 6 | 6 | 5 | 3 | 2 | 2 | 1 | BURROWS CROSS | | |
| 14 | 10 | 1/5 | 10 | 9 | 8 | 8 | 7 | 6 | 5 | 4 | 3 | 3 | 2 | 1½ | TORRELS | |
| 15 | 11 | 1/6 | 11 | 10 | 9 | 9 | 8 | 7 | 6 | 5 | 4 | 3 | 3 | 2 | 1 | PEASLAKE |
| | S | R | S | S | S | S | S | S | S | S | S | S | S | S | S | |

**Return tickets issued on "Tillingbourne Valley" buses are available for return on "London Transport" buses, and vice versa.**

S—Single fares (in light type). R—Return fares (in heavy type). RETURN TICKET HOLDERS have no precedence over other passengers, and no guarantee is given that they will be accommodated on any particular journey.
CHILDREN under 14, half fare, fractions of 1d. counting as 1d.
SMALL PARCELS will be carried on the Peaslake and Farley Green Routes at 6d. each, and on the Warren Road route at 2d. each, but cannot be accepted for points off the route, or if liable to cause delay.
LARGE DOGS AND PUSH-CHAIRS 2d. (or 1d. if fare is 2d. or less).

# CHAPTER 3 - A CHANGE OF COURSE

The services and the remaining GSs were sold to Trevor Wilcox Brown of Grayshott on 30 September 1970. Brown had become known to Derek Trice as far back as the early 1960s when the latter's firm was installing central heating equipment in some flats in Guildford owned by the Brown family. For a number of years, Brown had been dealing in buses and coaches and, with Tom Cadman, ran Astolat Coaches of Guildford, having aquired Bedford OB TMY 26 from Tillingbourne Valley back in September 1963. This coach was sometimes used for transporting volunteer workers to the fledgling National Tramways Museum at Crich in Derbyshire. Trevor Brown's family came from Guildford, where his father had run a food store, and for some years, Trevor Brown had worked in the oil industry. By 1970, his family operated a number of Wimpy fast-food franchises in West Surrey. The Trices' shares passed to Brown and his wife and the registered office of Tillingbourne Valley Services Ltd. was transferred to the Browns' Guildford business address at 27A Market Street, although vehicles were still garaged in Chilworth by a short term agreement with Derek Trice.

**32. The first vehicle purchased after the take over by Trevor Brown was JUO 982, an ex-Western National Bristol L-type with a lengthened chassis and full-front bus body. In 1971, clearance work for the Guildford town centre gyratory road scheme had started and the distinctive destination board-cum-clock at Farnham Road Bus station had already been demolished. (Authors Collection)**

Brown's first problem was the need to acquire urgently additional vehicles to replace some of the ailing GSs, and these initially consisted of a 1947 vintage former Royal Blue Bristol L6B coach from Western National, which had been rebodied by ECW in 1958 and lengthened to 30 feet with a full-fronted forward entrance bus body, and another GS, this time acquired from London Country. Early in 1971, a Bristol KSW6B lowbridge double decker arrived from Thames Valley, but this was not really suitable for operation on the bus services, except for short workings on the Guildford to Merrow section. The company was looking for a suitably economical vehicle type to replace the GSs, and the first attempt to achieve this was made early in 1971 when three secondhand Bristol SC4LK 35 seater ECW bodied buses were purchased. These vehicles, together with the L6B bus, were smartly painted into the maroon and grey Tillingbourne livery, with the attractive addition of the fleetname "TILLINGBOURNE VALLEY" in gold block letters of a similar style to that of certain NBC companies at that time. These vehicles also were equipped with three-track number blinds, which enabled the Peaslake route to be numbered 448, Farley Green 450 and Warren Road 451, being locally vacant numbers in London Country's numbering scheme.

Although the extra capacity of the SC4LK buses was welcome, and the four cylinder Gardner engines certainly economical, the vehicles were popular with neither the drivers nor the passengers as they were rough running and lacking in power, particularly when it came to the stiff climb up to Newlands Corner. Thus 1971 saw the arrival of further vehicles to replace the remaining GSs and these included an Albion Aberdonian, AEC Reliance and Daimler Roadliner coaches, another GS and several Bristol LS5Gs from Western National. The year also witnessed the introduction of a new fleet livery for the vehicles of light grey roof, yellow ochre waistband and Danube blue for the main body, the fleetname consisting of the word "Tillingbourne" in a slanted letter style. At the same time there was a partial replacement of Bell Punch type tickets with TIM ticket machines.

Since May 1950, two bus stations had been used at Guildford by local operators; that at Farnham Road was the terminus for Tillingbourne's Farley Green and Warren Road services, whilst on the other side of the River Wey and reached by footbridge, the Onslow Street Bus Station was the departure point for Peaslake and Pewley Way. Construction of a town centre traffic gyratory system necessitated the partial closure of the bus stations and, in April 1971, service 448 was allocated a temporary terminus at a stand in Commercial Road, whilst the 450 terminated in Millbrook outside Plummers Store (now Debenhams). Eventually the 448 route transferred to a small bus station constructed between Woodbridge Road and Commercial Road and the 450 moved to the re-opened Onslow Street site. From November 1980, all the various locations were replaced by the new Friary Bus Station, which includes stands on Commercial Road.

The Tillingbourne bus services had, by Summer 1971, passed the financial boundary from marginal profit to loss, and the withdrawal of services 450 and 451 was threatened from 18 July 1971 unless some form of outside support was forthcoming. No action was taken pending the result of discussions with Surrey County Council for financial assistance, although, as a desparate measure, a 16 seater Ford Transit vehicle was tried on the route 451 service in early October. However the County Council declined to support the Warren Road route on the grounds that it was a town rather than a rural route. Thus service 451 was abandoned from 16 October, but local public protest prompted the Guildford firm Safeguard Coaches to provide a limited replacement service from 25 October. It was for a ten week trial period, but poor patronage led to its inevitable withdrawal on 18 December. The lower half of Warren Road was to be served from March 1973 by a new route between the town centre and Boxgrove Park operated by the Blue Saloon company (ABC Taxis). The 448 and 450 services gained revised timetables on 23 October 1971, which avoided the need for immediate County financial support; on 450 all Sunday buses were withdrawn.

**33. The first double decker owned was an ex-Thames Valley Bristol KSW6B. It saw some use on service 448, attractively painted into maroon and grey livery. It is seen here in the yard at New Road, Chilworth in the 1970/71 winter. (J.Gaff)**

Other important changes were taking place in the organisation of one of the local NBC operators at this time. On 1 January 1972, the former British Electric Traction subsidiary, the Aldershot and District Traction Company, was merged with the former Tilling subsidiary, the Thames Valley Traction Company to form the Thames Valley and Aldershot Omnibus Company, to be better known by its trading name of Alder Valley. It would not be unfair to say that the merger of these two companies, with their dissimilar policies on many matters, was to be a long drawn

**34. Three Bristol SC4LK s arrived in early 1971 to replace GSs, two from Eastern Counties and this one from Crosville. The availability of three-track number blinds meant that the routes could be numbered. 790 EFM arrives from Farley Green at the partially-demolished Farnham Road Bus Station. (D.Stuttard)**

**35. 170 BUP was a Willowbrook-bodied Albion Aberdonian acquired from Venture Transport of Consett, Co. Durham. It lasted only three months with Tillingbourne and was photographed in Commercial Road, Guildford awaiting departure for Peaslake. (J.Gaff)**

out and somewhat painful process which would have a direct effect on service quality in the Guildford area for the remainder of the 1970s, although none of this was evident in early 1972.

**36. MXX 364 was the last GS owned and was one of the first vehicles to carry the new blue, grey and yellow livery. Although seen here in North Street, Guildford, it spent much of its last few months working route 451 from Horsham to Rusper. (J.Gaff)**

Derek Trice had leased the premises at 126 New Road, Chilworth to Tillingbourne Valley Services Ltd. for one year, and having exceeded this period, the company was forced to seek alternative premises, which were not easy to find. Guildford Borough Council offered a site at Slyfield Industrial Estate on the northern outskirts of Guildford, but this was turned down for operational reasons. An agreement was reached with British Rail to lease part of the Station Yard at Gomshall for vehicle parking, the station buildings having previously been demolished. No planning permission existed for additional structures and maintenance had to be carried out in the open, although a pit was constructed. The Station Yard was also used for dealing activities in buses and coaches, which Trevor Brown carried out as T.Brown Transport Sales. He also used premises near the Aldershot & District Depot at Hindhead. Some of the vehicles involved found their way into the operational Tillingbourne fleet for short periods, before being resold. With the reduced maintenance facilities available, the reliability of the bus routes was suffering a severe decline, and it must have been tempting to draft in such vehicles from the dealing stock if they had any time left on their "tickets", although this resulted in a poor image of the company to the travelling public. An attempt was made to develop some private hire activities and a school contract was gained; these activities took vehicles and drivers away from the stage services, another factor which contributed to unreliability and the subsequent loss of patronage.

The winter of 1971/72 probably witnessed the nadir of Tillingbourne's fortunes. Receipts from the bus services were still declining owing to unreliable operation, the manager appointed by Brown in 1970 had left and the company's expanded activities severely stretched available staff and vehicle resources. Breakdowns were regular occurances and the school contract had been lost. In March 1972 Barry King, who had gained his bus operating experience with London Transport and London Country Bus Services, was appointed full-time manager and it is fair to say that this marked the beginning of the upturn in the company's fortunes and it began to evolve slowly into the type of operation it is today.

**37. Apart from the application of a fleetname, AEC Reliance/Harrington 645 WKX remained in the livery of its former owner Keith's Coaches of Aylesbury. The first 36 footer in the fleet, its 51 seat capacity reduced the need for peak hour duplication on busy journeys. (J.Gaff)**

Another operator in the area was at that time experiencing financial and vehicle maintenance problems. North Downs Rural Transport could not persuade Surrey County Council to offer revenue support to its services, and it abruptly terminated its operations on 17 April 1972 after prohibition notices were served on its vehicles by a Ministry Inspector, and the company could not afford to repair them. It was not until 24 April that Forest Green garage owner Tony McCann was able to restart service 845 along the Tillingbourne Valley, initially operating "on hire" to North Downs until he secured licences of his own for the services at a Traffic

**38. One of several Bristol LS5G's purchased from Western National was MOD 954, seen at Commercial Road, Guildford in 1971. This vehicle subsequently passed to North Downs Rural Transport and still appeared in Guildford on their service 845 from Forest Green. (D.Stuttard)**

Commissioners Hearing in June of that year. Both Tillingbourne and London Country had unsuccessfully tried to prevent his take over of the erstwhile North Downs services from Forest Green, whilst an application by Blue Saloon to acquire route 845 was withdrawn before the Hearing. McCann resurrected "Brown Motor Services" as a trading name and, until a bus-bodied Bedford SB8 vehicle could be put into traffic on the Guildford service, he had a petrol-engined Bedford coach on long-term hire from Tillingbourne, despite the latter's opposition to his activities.

Barry King had previously left the relative security of employment with London Country to take up the challenge of helping to manage the North Downs concern, however it was clear to him by March 1972 that North Downs was in some financial difficulty. Consequently, it must have been an agreeable solution when Trevor Brown, anxious to recruit a competent full time manager, made an offer that Barry should join Tillingbourne. As though anticipating the events of 17 April, North Downs had, three days previously, given notice that their circular route 851 from Horsham to Rusper and Colgate would cease to operate on that date. Following hurried negotiations with West Sussex County Council, which offered a £1,000 subsidy per annum, Tillingbourne assumed operation of the route and renumbered it 451. Also acquired as part of the 451 was a one-way Monday to Friday journey from Horsham to Broadbridge Heath and Warnham. After a short time the vehicle used on this service began to be out-stationed overnight in Horsham, and this was

**39. Ex-Western National LS5G LTA 988 waits at the temporary terminus of route 450 in Millbrook, Guildford outside Plummers Department Store, whilst construction work was taking place at Farnham Road Bus Station. (J.Gaff)**

**40. Trevor Brown is seen at the wheel of KDD 275E, a rear-engined Daimler Roadliner/Plaxton coach purchased from Black & White Motorways of Cheltenham. The location is the station yard at Gomshall and the shelter in the background had replaced the original station buildings. (L.Smith)**

initially an ex-Western National Bristol SUL4A or the last GS owned, MXX 364, which looked very smart in the new blue, yellow and grey livery. Tillingbourne bought three SUL4As at this time, principally for use on the 450 and 451, whilst some ex-London Transport RF-type vehicles and an ex-Red and White Bristol LS6G were used on the 448, replacing the earlier LSs and the SC4LKs. The SUL4As gave good service, being both nippy and economical buses, as did the RFs and the number of Leyland Tiger Cub vehicles which were purchased over the following two years.

**41. A youthful Barry King watches passengers board ex-London Transport RF649, NLE 699 at Commercial Road. The London Country Leyland Atlantean double decker in the background had then recently been delivered to replace the famous RT-type vehicles on route 408. (L.Smith)**

The new manager implemented revised timetables for services 448 and 450 to utilise more effectively the available staff and vehicle resources. On the 448, a timetable which came into effect on 24 April 1972 retained weekday evening and Sunday afternoon journeys at the request of Surrey County Council, which conducted its own survey to establish demand and to decide whether it should offer financial support. The results showed that usage was minimal, and evening and Sunday journeys were subsequently withdrawn. The Saturday afternoon service was reduced from two to one bus operation and service 450 was retimed on a more regular headway. Journeys between Albury Park and Farley Green in one direction were diverted via Brook level crossing, passengers for Little London travelling via Farley Green at no extra charge. Both Guildford routes were passed for the operation of 11 metre one-man operated vehicles, indeed, surprisingly, the 448 was

**42. NLE 595, ex-RF 595 looks in need of a wash as it waits to leave for Peaslake. Notice how the LT bullseye motif on the front has been suitably altered! (J.Gaff)**

**43. Ex-Thames Valley Bristol LD6B LWN 52 started life with United Welsh. It saw some use on service 448 between Guildford and Gomshall and a crew change is occurring at the latter location probably early in 1972. (J.Gaff)**

**44. Bedford SB3 coach YUE 163 was seen on the Peaslake route before going on long-term loan to Brown Motor Services (McCann) of Forest Green, being the regular vehicle on route 845 between April and August 1972. (J.Gaff)**

**45. New to A.T. Brady's Brown Motor Services, Bedford VAS1/Marshall Cambrette 3255 PJ passed through the hands of North Downs Rural Transport before arriving with Tillingbourne in January 1972. repainted blue and cream, it was used in service for a short time before becoming a seat store at Gomshall yard. (D.Stuttard)**

approved for double deck operation, although the Bristol Lodekka LD6D purchased to replace the KSW6B vehicle rarely if ever worked the section between Gomshall and Peaslake. The use of larger vehicles meant that peak hour duplicates could be withdrawn. The County Council, however, still declined to offer financial support for the services, other than ad hoc payments made to continue evening and Sunday services while demand for these was investigated.

By May 1972, the company was using the name Tillingbourne Bus Co. Ltd., as with an expanded area of operation the old name was deemed to be inappropriate, however the official change of title does not seem to have occurred until August 1972. The Government's policy of offering grant aid to operators to enable them to purchase new vehicles for stage carriage use was taken advantage of by Tillingbourne, who took delivery in June 1972 of its first new vehicle since 1946 - a 47 seater Bedford YRQ with Willowbrook bus body registered LPD 12 K. This was a landmark in the Company's history, as in each subsequent year at least one new vehicle has been purchased, enabling the fleet to be totally modernised. On the bus services, the previous ticketing arrangements were replaced by secondhand Setright equipment.

Situated slightly away from the Guildford - Merrow section of service 448, the private housing development of Boxgrove Park Estate attracted Tillingbourne's attention as offering some commercial potential. After discussing the use of minibuses with the Ford Motor Co., Tillingbourne proposed a Dial-a-Ride service for both Boxgrove Park and the Warren Road area, to terminate outside Guildford Station for rail connections. British Rail would not consider this, and strong opposition from other operators and local taxi firms meant that plans were re-formulated on a more limited scale for an off-peak shopping service on Mondays to Fridays, with Warren Road being included to appease the local council rather than in the hope of increased profitability compared to the erstwhile 451 service. A competing application was made by Blue Saloon Coaches for a daily Guildford - Boxgrove Park route, and London Country proposed to divert their 408A Guildford to Merrow, Bushy Hill service. At the Traffic Court Hearing, Blue Saloon won the day as the Commissioner felt that their service was the more suitable as it also ran on Sundays for hospital visiting at St.Lukes.

By the end of 1972, the economies made by Tillingbourne were beginning to pay off and bus service receipts were improving as passenger confidence was restored. The Company was convinced that its future welfare would best be achieved by obtaining new vehicles, which would significantly decrease maintenance costs and enhance the image of the services, and thus, hopefully, the patronage. However, the Company was unable to obtain the necessary finance, and, consequently, in December 1972, Barry King wrote to Surrey County Council suggesting that, under the terms of the 1968 Transport Act, the Council should advance the Company an interest free loan of some £16,500 in order to purchase three new vehicles. This sum represented 50% of the amount needed, the balance would have been obtained from central government bus grant and the advantage to the Council would have been a guarantee to operate the services without any further financial support for a period of five years. The County Council gave serious consideration to this idea, but rejected it in favour of more conventional methods of support and, as it was claimed that a slight loss was still being made on services 448 and 450, an application

**46. Three of these 36 seat Bristol SUL4As were purchased from Western National in 1972 and were ideal for rural bus work, being fitted with economical four-cylinder Albion engines. 347 EDV leaves Guildford for Peaslake. (J.Gaff)**

**47. The other two SULs are seen parked in Horsham Goods Yard, ready for use on route 451, one of their regular haunts. (L.Smith)**

was made again to the County Council early in 1973 for revenue support grant under section 34 of the 1968 Transport Act, and this was eventually approved on 25 September 1973. With the future looking brighter, thoughts were again turned towards the private hire market and further vehicles of dual-purpose nature were purchased by the grant-aid scheme to enable them to be used on bus work during the week and on coaching duties at weekends, which on Summer Saturdays often meant acting as "National Express" duplicates. In January 1973 came NPH 33 L, a Willowbrook Expressway 002 coach-bodied Leyland Leopard which became a regular performer on one of the two school contracts which the Company subsequently successfully tendered for. More secondhand vehicles arrived and a new Leyland Leopard/Plaxton bodied coach was ordered. This vehicle would have been registered ORO 330 M, but delivery delays meant the order was cancelled and PWY 595 M, a Bedford YRT/Duple Dominant bodied coach was purchased from dealer's stock, with ORO 330 M finally going to Silcox of Pembroke Dock.

**48. MAX 134 originated with Red & White but had been owned by Gosport & Fareham Omnibus Co. (Provincial) before Tillingbourne purchased it in May 1972, primarily for use on service 448. It was a Bristol LS6G with 39 seat ECW coach body previously downgraded for local bus work. (Authors Collection)**

Tillingbourne now had two separate areas of operation:- the traditional Guildford/Peaslake/Farley Green routes and the circular service at Horsham. The need for interchanging vehicles resulted in a fair amount of dead mileage, and to obviate this and to create some new links for shoppers into Horsham and Guildford, application was made in March 1973 to extend two 448 journeys on Tuesdays beyond Peaslake to Horsham via Ewhurst, Walliswood, Oakwoodhill, Ockley, Capel, Kingsfold, Warnham and Broadbridge Heath. An objection was lodged by McCann's Brown Motor Services, which already ran a Tuesday service between Forest Green and Horsham via some of these points, a route which had been inherited from North Downs. In May there was a Traffic Court Hearing at which Tillingbourne was granted dispensation to operate the extension on Thursdays, when McCann did not operate. It commenced on 21 June, being numbered 449. However, at the Hearing for the new application to run on Thursdays, the Traffic Commissioners refused to grant a full licence on the grounds of insufficient need and similarly dismissed a counter-application by McCann to operate into Horsham on Thursdays. Accordingly, service 449 was withdrawn on 12 July, and the Company's two areas remained separate for the time being.

**49. Another brief flirtation with a double decker came in the form of SOU 454, a Dennis Loline 1 which started life with Aldershot & District. When seen in Shere in 1972, the original LT "bullseye" bus stop signs had not yet been replaced by the standard DoT.- approved design for use outside of London. Barry King is also featured in this view. (Authors Collection)**

From 7 July, as part of a re-organisation of routes in the Dorking area, London Country extended journeys on service 425 from Dorking to Brockham, Leigh, Reigate and Redhill, whilst service 439 was revised to run as a circular from Dorking to Brockham, Parkgate, Newdigate, Beare Green and South Holmwood, before

**50. The first new vehicle purchased since 1946 was LPD 12K, a Bedford YRQ with Willowbrook bus body which arrived in June 1972. About a year later it was at the Hurtwood Inn, Peaslake on the short-lived through service from Horsham to Guildford numbered 449. (B.LeJeune)**

**51. Bus Grant obtained from central Government was used to purchase new dual-purpose vehicles, which had to perform a certain quota of stage carriage work. This Leyland Leopard with angular Willowbrook Expressway 002 body was also regularly used on school contracts, private hire and as a National Express duplicate. (Authors Collection)**

proceeding to Guildford along the 425 route. An hourly frequency was maintained along the Dorking - Guildford section, rising to half-hourly Mondays to Fridays during the afternoon and early evening and on Saturdays.

These services, of course, paralleled parts of Tillingbourne services 448 and 450,

**52. One of a pair of Leyland Tiger Cubs acquired in June 1973 from Pennine Motor Services was 6108 WU, which received exterior advertising for Bill McAllister's mobile homes business which operated from the premises seen at the rear of this view of Gomshall station yard. (H.Retallick)**

and in 1972/73 timings of each company's journeys sometimes co-incided, leading to buses racing each other to stops and London Country complained to the Metropolitan Traffic Commissioners about the supposed late-running of Tillingbourne buses on service 450. In an attempt to improve relationships, negotiations were held between the parties which led to the introduction of a revised timetable on route 450 which allowed for improved interworking with 425 between Albury and Guildford. The changes occurred in January 1974 and included the diversion of one trip each way at Chilworth Station to double-run to Blackheath, giving that hamlet its first bus service since 1955.

Mainly for accounting reasons, a wholly-owned subsidiary company with a nominal £100 capital, Tillingbourne (Sussex) Ltd. was set up in May 1974 to administer the Horsham area 451 route. Initially, Leyland Tiger Cub 9712 WX and Bristol SUL4A 269 KTA were licenced to it. Since then, some of the fleet have always been licenced to the Sussex subsidiary, but these vehicles and those of the main fleet have always operated indiscriminately on all routes.

The yard at Gomshall only allowed open-air maintenance of vehicles, although the Company had an arrangement with a haulage firm at Witley to use its workshop, but this was over ten miles away. The management, learning from its own experience and that of other local companies, was determined to ensure that maintenance standards were of the highest, despite these conditions. For some years after the takeover of the North Downs Horsham service, the regular driver of the 451 was Charlie Bowler, who had previously been a driver with both Tom Brady and North Downs, and in 1973 his son, Chris, was employed to look after the maintenance of the fleet. Despite less than ideal conditions, significant improvements soon resulted until the highest standards were reached and maintained right through to the present day.

Nevertheless, the task of finding suitable premises was the most pressing problem facing the Company in the 1973/74 period. Potential sites were inspected at Slyfield Industrial Estate, Holmwood, Horsham and Woking amongst others, but none were deemed to be suitable. The problem became acute when Guildford Rural District Council served an enforcement order to prevent Tillingbourne using the Station Yard at Gomshall, as the land concerned was deemed to be within the "Green Belt" and no planning permission had been obtained. Brown's bus dealing activities, although they had virtually ceased by 1974, had also upset local residents and the Council. An appeal was lodged by the Company and it entered into abortive negotiations for the lease of some property in Shere. A planning application by the Company for a garage and office at the Station Yard was refused, and to replace the wooden shed used as an office which had had to be demolished, a small wooden building in Station Approach was rented from the adjacent McAllister mobile home business. The Company appeared before Guildford magistrates in February 1974 for failing to comply with the enforcement notice, which had originally been issued in July 1972, and was fined a nominal sum of £50. This enforcement notice required the discontinuance of the use of the Station Yard as a depot for motor vehicles and for the storage, inspection, maintenance and repair of motor vehicles. Failure to comply meant that Tillingbourne faced a possible fine of £50 for each day the Company remained at Gomshall, however the newly created Guildford Borough Council, whilst anxious to have the Company vacate the Station Yard, was more constructive in its approach compared with the old Rural District Council and was prepared to allow the Company more time to secure alternative premises. Nevertheless, in March 1974, British Rail informed Tillingbourne that, owing to pressure from the local authority, the Company must vacate the site immediately. Unable to operate without a base, London Country was sounded out in desperation concerning a possible takeover. The latter was prepared to make an offer equivalent to the assets, but not taking into account any "goodwill". Tillingbourne found this unacceptable and took the decision to carry on operating from Gomshall.

Ewhurst Coaches used a small depot in The Street at Ewhurst, a building originally erected by George Readings for his Surrey Hills business in the early 1920s. It had passed through the hands of Aldershot and District and London Transport, although the latter did not use it, and was eventually sold to the Lazzell family who sold Ewhurst Coaches to Gastonia Coaches Ltd. in 1971. Financial assistance to enable the purchase of the garage was sought by Tillingbourne from Guildford and Hambledon Councils in February 1974, but the latter authority, and its successor, Waverley District Council, felt that the site was unsuitable for buses as it was situated in the centre of a village in a conservation area, on land affected

**53. At Horsham Carfax on route 451 to Rusper was 269 KTA, another ex-Western National SUL4A, but with coach seats. It was one of the first two vehicles to be licensed to the Tillingbourne(Sussex) subsidiary. (Authors Collection)**

**54. Owing to delivery delays on a Leyland Leopard/Plaxton coach, this Duple-bodied Bedford YRT was purchased from dealer's stock in January 1974 and is here performing on a Private Hire for a party of American tourists. (G.Burnett)**

by "Green Belt" policies. Undaunted, the purchase was pursued and Trevor Brown bought the garage in his own name in October 1974 and then leased it to the Tillingbourne Company.

As Guildford Borough Council had decided to wait on events with regard to the purchase of the Ewhurst Depot, which had first been proposed by Tillingbourne in February 1974, British Rail had not implemented their notice to quit Gomshall Station Yard. Following the purchase of the Ewhurst premises, Tillingbourne applied to Waverley District Council for an Established User Certificate and planning permission to extend the premises in order to accommodate the size of vehicles operated by the Company, which were, of course, considerably larger than those used by previous occupants of the premises. However Waverley District Council had come under much local pressure to prevent any use of the Ewhurst Depot, let alone to permit an extension which was considered to be out of character with the rural nature of the village. Thus, yet again, the Company's ability to continue operating its services from a suitable base seemed to be balanced on a knife's edge.

With Guildford Borough Council taking the view that, having purchased the Ewhurst premises, Tillingbourne should be in a position to vacate Gomshall Station Yard, and with the strong likelihood that the Company would fail in its attempt to obtain an Established User Certificate and permission to build an extension from Waverley District Council, Surrey County Council was becoming increasingly alarmed at the possibility of Tillingbourne having to cease operations, with all the difficulties and expense of securing alternative services. Consequently, the County decided to act as a mediator and arranged a meeting for all the interested parties on 3 February 1975.

At this meeting, Guildford Borough Council continued to express their objections to Tillingbourne's presence at Gomshall, whilst Waverley explained that, although the application to build an extension was unlikely to be approved, the Council might be prepared to allow three named vehicles to be garaged and maintained at Ewhurst, but certainly not the full fleet of eight vehicles. Barry King stated that the preferred solution for the Company would be to park five vehicles at Gomshall and three at Ewhurst, with vehicles being rotated into Ewhurst for maintenance purposes. Further difficulties arose when the representative of British Rail, although very sympathetic to the Company's plight, announced that final notice to quit Gomshall would be effective the next day unless Guildford Borough Council were prepared to change their minds. In response, Barry King stated that, were the Company to be ejected from Gomshall Station Yard, the five vehicles would immediately be parked in Shere High Street. Surrey County Council took the view that, as both Guildford and Waverley recognised the important part played by the Company in the provision of rural bus services, they both had an obligation to assist the Company in carrying out its business. Thus, although the meeting seemed inconclusive, the representatives of the two districts went away to report to their respective committees, and all actions were suspended pending the decisions of these committees.

On 11 February 1975, Guildford Borough Council's Planning Committee agreed to allow Tillingbourne to park five vehicles at Gomshall Station Yard, provided that no maintenance of any sort was carried out and that the parking space was in a

**55. VCH 172, a Leyland Tiger Cub/Willowbrook dual-purpose vehicle which started life with Trent Motor Traction, sets down in North Street, Guildford opposite the "Horse and Groom" which became an I.R.A. bomb target, as it was often frequented by military personnel. (N.Hamshere)**

**56. The current Managing Director of the company, Chris Bowler, was driving in this view of Bedford YRQ/Plaxton GPA 846N, seen passing through Shalford. Note the incorrect route number displayed! (N.Hamshere)**

different area to that still subject to the Enforcement Notice. However, Waverley District Council, on 4 February, refused planning permission for an extension and office accommodation at Ewhurst. Nevertheless, as the Company then appealed to the Secretary of State, a breathing space was created to see whether an acceptable compromise could be reached. On 9 June, a meeting took place between officers and members of Waverley District Council and the County Council and officers of Guildford Borough Council to consider the matter further. Despite opposition from the District Council member who represented Ewhurst, a compromise was agreed whereby the District Council would establish the existing use rights for the Ewhurst garage site and would also consider a planning application for a temporary extension, while the County Council's Transportation Planning Unit would enter into discussions with Tillingbourne to sound out the possibility of the Company being prepared to move in the longer term to a suitable shared site in the Cranleigh area. As this "temporary" solution was to be allowed for three years, and as Tillingbourne were still confident of winning their appeal to the Secretary of State, the matter was allowed to rest with the Company feeling more secure than had been the case for some years, however the premises saga was far from over.

On the operations side, as a result of the move of some of the Company's vehicles to Ewhurst, from February 1975 the Horsham bus was timetabled to run from Ewhurst via Forest Green, Ockley and Capel to join the 451 proper at Rusper, working in reverse at the end of the day.

Great progress had also been made in upgrading the state of the vehicle fleet. From 1972, the fleet size had stabilised at 8 to 9 vehicles, and was to remain at this size until the late 1970s. In October 1974, a further new vehicle in the shape of GPA 846 N, a Bedford YRQ bus with Plaxton Derwent 45 seat body, was delivered. This proved to be a very useful, reliable and well-built bus and, consequently, Plaxton bodywork was to be favoured for many years to come. At the end of 1972, the fleet consisted of one vehicle purchased new, and eight purchased secondhand with an average age of twelve years. Chassis types operated were AEC Regal IV, AEC Reliance, Bristol LS, Bristol SUL, Daimler Roadliner and Bedford YRQ, with bodywork by Metro-Cammell, ECW, Willowbrook, Plaxton and Harrington. By the end of 1974, the total number of vehicles purchased new had risen to four, with a further four second hand machines. Chassis types were Bristol SUL, Bedford YRQ and YRT, Leyland Tiger Cub and Leyland Leopard with bodywork by ECW, Willowbrook, Duple and Plaxton, all with an average age reduced to seven years. At this stage it was the intention to have a fleet mix of lightweight Bedfords purchased new and heavyweight Leylands, either purchased new or selected secondhand stock.

# CHAPTER 4 - A NEW IMAGE

At last Tillingbourne had managed to obtain proper premises for the maintenance of its fleet, and it is well worth pausing to consider the changes which had occurred in the period 1970 to 1974. After the near disasters of 1971/72, the Company had managed a quite remarkable turnaround in its fortunes. By concentrating on providing a reliable bus service, at a time when many of its larger neighbours were struggling badly in this respect, and by cutting out the severe loss-making parts of the network, both loadings and revenue had increased to the point where the services were sustainable into the future. Other activities were started in a systematic fashion, with the intention of increasing profitability and providing a firm platform for possible future expansion. School contracts were operated, and these were soon to be integrated into the stage carriage network, either by using vehicles which were engaged on the normal all-day bus schedules, or by developing new off-peak services which would enhance the revenue earned per vehicle. A further regular source of income was considered to be necessary, and initially this had consisted of working duplicate summer services for National Express, an activity shared by many other small independent operators. By 1974, the Company had started to tender for weekend rail replacement services with both British Rail and London Transport, and continued success in this field was to be a significant factor throughout the rest of the 1970s and early 1980s.

1975 was largely a year of consolidation, however, by utilising the vehicle which performed a school contract to the Weald School at Billingshurst, a new shoppers service 452 was provided at little cost from February 1975. It consisted of one return journey on Fridays from Wisborough Green to Cranleigh via Loxwood and Alfold, and to gain more patronage it was diverted the following August between Wisborough Green and Loxwood via Kirdford and Plaistow. During the summer of 1975, the increasing costs of revenue support for London Country route 432, which operated between Guildford and Bookham Station via Merrow, East Clandon, West Horsley, East Horsley and Effingham was causing concern for Surrey County Council, and Tillingbourne put forward a proposal to take over the operation of this service from London Country. Matters progressed sufficiently that destination blinds for the 432 service appeared in the new Bedford bus delivered at that time, however the County Council eventually decided to negotiate changes with the incumbent operator.

In October 1975, an application was made for a service designed to take shoppers on the first and third Wednesdays of each month to the West Sussex county town of Chichester. Starting at Kirdford, it was intended to run via Wisborough Green, Billingshurst, Pulborough, Bury, Bignor, Sutton and Duncton. During school holidays, Alfold, Loxwood and Plaistow would also be served. This encroachment onto Southdown's traditional territory prompted that operator to apply for two routes: 288 Kirdford to Chichester on Fridays, and 289 Kirdford to Brighton on Wednesdays. Tillingbourne's first attempt to serve Chichester was not favoured by the Traffic Commissioners, but Southdown's applications were granted and the services commenced in February 1976.

**57. Another pair of vehicles was acquired from Pennine of Gargrave in 1975, being sturdy Roe-bodied Leyland Leopards 240 CWY and LWU 499D. The latter is seen in Commercial Road, Guildford on service 448. (N.Hamshere)**

**58. The small bus garage in the main street in Ewhurst was originally used by George Readings for his Surrey Hills Motor Services business in the early 1920's. It was acquired by Tillingbourne in 1974 for maintenance purposes and was used until premises in Cranleigh became available. Parts of it are now incorporated into a replica bus garage at the Amberley Chalk Pits Museum. (L.James)**

Bearing in mind the rural nature of Tillingbourne's services, together with the fact that the most highly used sections of route were shared with one or more other operators, it was obviously necessary for the Company to think in terms of expansion wherever possible, although this posed many problems in trying not to upset unduly relations with neighbouring operators and local authorities, acting in their transport co-ordinating role. Significant steps in the expansion of the Company's bus network took place in 1976, both in Surrey and in West Sussex. It will be recalled that, on taking over sole operation of the 448 service from London Transport, the section of route between Ewhurst and Peaslake was soon abandoned by Tillingbourne. Ewhurst was not a significant destination in itself, and residents of the village were well served by the regular Alder Valley service to Guildford via Cranleigh. However, the village of Cranleigh was developing very rapidly and becoming a popular local shopping centre, particularly with the elderly, who appreciated the flat nature of the terrain compared with Guildford's hilly streets. Tillingbourne had received several enquiries from passengers concerning the possibility of running from Peaslake to Cranleigh, and with the location of the Tillingbourne Garage in Ewhurst, this became an attractive proposition.

Consequently, on 3 May 1976, with the approval of Surrey County Council, a new timetable was introduced which included the extension of five return journeys per day (four on Saturdays) beyond Peaslake to Cranleigh. At the same time, by utilising a school contract, a facility was provided each schoolday from a small hamlet called The Haven, which had previously never had a bus service, and Rudgwick to Guildford via Ewhurst and the 448 routeing. In fact the original intention was to operate the service from Billingshurst and Five Oaks, but this idea was dropped. Although all Alder Valley stops between Cranleigh and Ewhurst were served, passengers were not carried locally between Ewhurst and Cranleigh or between Bucks Green and Ellens Green in order to protect Alder Valley from revenue abstraction. An attractive leaflet was produced extolling the virtues of the new service, among which were claimed to be fast direct links from Cranleigh/ Ewhurst to Peaslake, Gomshall, Shere and St.Lukes Hospital, train connections at Gomshall and easy to remember departure times from Guildford (usually at 51 minutes past the hour), the travelling public being exhorted to travel by the Tillingbourne Blue Buses, their local independent company. Examination of the timetable shows that the different bus services and school contract runs were scheduled to be interworked to maximise efficiency, as opposed to previous practice where each route tended to be totally self-contained.

In September of that year, the Horsham service was revised in the light of changing travel patterns. Usage had declined from the villages of Colgate and Rusper, however new housing developments on the northern outskirts of Horsham in the area of North Heath Lane had created additional demand, and the timetable for service 451 was altered to allow for this. The majority of journeys were diverted to operate along North Heath Lane instead of Pondtail Road and there was a small increase in their number. Additionally, the journey to Warnham was also diverted via North Heath Lane, and thence via Warnham Station. The peak hour Rusper journeys were extended to and from Forest and Millais Schools in Horsham, which enabled West Sussex County Council to cancel a school contract and was most useful in enhancing the revenue for Tillingbourne. The new schedule was still able to be operated by one driver, and there was no significant decline in the service provided to the rural areas, however it was a portent of things to come in the Horsham operation.

In December 1976, the result of Tillingbourne's appeal to the Secretary of State regarding the refusal of Waverley District Council to grant planning permission for an extension to the garage at Ewhurst was published. Unfortunately, the appeal was dismissed, however, as the Company had by now been granted an Established User Certificate, it was able to continue the use of the existing facilities, inadequate although they were.

During this period, two new Bedford vehicles were delivered, in 1975 came LPE 42 P, a Plaxton Supreme 45 seat coach and in 1976 MPE 248 P, to all intents identical to GPA 846 N. Notable secondhand purchases in 1975 were two Leyland Leopard buses with Roe bodywork from the fleet of Pennine Motor Services of Gargrave. The Leyland Leopard delivered new in 1973, NPH 33 L, had not been a conspicuous success, as its bodywork did not seem able to stand up to the ravages of rural bus operation, consequently it was sold somewhat prematurely in 1976. By the end of 1976, the fleet had become significantly more standardised, consisting of five Bedford "Y" type vehicles all purchased new, and three secondhand Leopards further reducing the average age of the fleet to five years.

Mention has been made above of how, in a way reminiscent of the erstwhile Surrey Hills concern, Tillingbourne made much play of the connections available at Gomshall Station with British Rail services. During 1976 and 1977, several leaflets were published in conjunction with British Rail which were entitled "Road and Rail Timetables" and which included full details of the local rail services. By coincidence, at this time Tillingbourne were regularly operating the rail replacement service on Sundays on the Reading to Tonbridge line, particularly on the stretch from Redhill to Tonbridge. Familiarity with Sunday rail operation seems to have led to the Company applying for a licence to operate the Sunday service from Edenbridge to Westerham via Holland, Hurst Green, Oxted and Limpsfield, extending to Chartwell via Hosey Common in the summer period, when Sunday services were under threat of withdrawal by British Rail in 1976. However, with the continuation of Sunday rail services, the application was withdrawn.

In April 1977, two new off-peak services were commenced which were of some interest. Route 453 operated a return trip every Tuesday between Cranleigh and Croydon via Ewhurst, Forest Green, Ockley, Capel, Newdigate, Strood Green, Brockham, Reigate, Coulsdon and Purley, while route 454 operated the first Wednesday of every month between Ewhurst (connecting with the 448 service bus from Guildford) and Chichester, via Cranleigh, Alfold, Loxwood, Plaistow, Mackerels Common and Petworth. The difficulties encountered in starting such modest services and the slowness of the licencing system before the implementation of the 1985 Transport Act are demonstrated by the fact that the original application for the Chichester service was made in May 1976, and that for Croydon (originally to be numbered 449) in November 1976, yet neither service could start before April 1977. Subsequent objections from Alder Valley, Southdown and London Country led to numerous amendments and restrictions in the ability to carry passengers locally and the long delay in the start of the services to April 1977.

Interestingly, Surrey and West Sussex County Councils were looking between them at the bus service provision in the Billingshurst, Plaistow and Cranleigh area during 1977, and Tillingbourne produced a report for the benefit of the two county councils reviewing its various off-peak rural services in that area. The Report concerns itself with the marginally costed off-peak services 452, 453 and 454, together with the extension of service 448 to Cranleigh. These services were typical of several that Tillingbourne introduced during the later 1970s and 1980s as the Company continually sought enhanced revenue from its regular stage carriage operations and a good yield from the infrequent marginally costed routes.

**59. Being licensed to the Sussex subsidiary company, LPE 42P spent a lot of time working route 451 at Horsham. A Bedford YRQ with Plaxton Supreme body, it is seen at Peaslake on an Omnibus Society tour in 1976. It was later exported to Cyprus. (MB Transport Photos)**

The Report told how an intensive publicity campaign was mounted prior to the introduction of route 452, with house to house distribution in the most crucial areas, a move typical of most subsequent Tillingbourne new services. Following the introduction of the service in February 1975, the load carried averaged 30 passengers, although the section via Roundstreet Common was poorly patronised, hence the re-routeing via Plaistow and Ifold mentioned previously. Such was the demand on the first day of operation of the revised service, that a duplicate vehicle had to be provided! However, as was the case with most similar services, the loads carried steadied at a lower figure once the novelty value had worn off, and by 1977, service 452 was carrying 30 to 40 passengers per week, rising to 50 to 60 in the school holidays. A glowing account of the service was conveyed, however the sting in the tail came with the concern expressed over the proposed diversion of Alder Valley service 269 on Tuesdays and Thursdays with its obvious detrimental effect on the pioneering Tillingbourne service.

The success of the 453 Croydon service was far less sure, with loadings varying from 15 to 40, with the Company finding it particularly difficult to disseminate publicity effectively over such a scattered area. Nevertheless, the Report showed confidence in the future of the route, which was, unfortunately, misplaced as the service was withdrawn rather abruptly in September the same year, although the reason given for this was the difficulty of covering the service following the acquisition of some lucrative private hire work for the Sayers Croft Rural Studies Centre at Ewhurst, which was owned by the Inner London Education Authority. The Chichester service 454 was an undoubted success, as is demonstrated by the loading figures which started at 29 on the first day of operation, rose to the mid-50s and peaked in August when two vehicles were needed to carry the total load of 110 passengers! From October 1977, service 454 was increased to twice monthly.

The Report detailed the history behind the 448 extension to Cranleigh, mentioned in passing the contribution made by Surrey County Council of £500 for the first year of operation and detailed the results of passenger surveys. The service was deemed to be fairly successful, although it was admitted that the promised use of the service from the Peaslake area had failed to materialise, nevertheless a plea was made for its continued support as a socially necessary service and for the restrictions in force between Ewhurst and Cranleigh to be lifted. The Report concluded that all services had demonstrated trip generation and ended with a plea for the production of a comprehensive County or area timetable for the benefit of both passengers and operators.

On a more negative note, July 1977 saw the withdrawal of the school days only extensions of service 448 to The Haven as a result of a change in school contracts. Following the withdrawal in many parts of the country of rural evening services in the early 1970s, a concept which enjoyed a temporary vogue at this time was that of a specialist limited evening service, targetted at specific attractions in the local town (such as the cinema) and operated to a more flexible timetable and routeing than traditional evening services. Tillingbourne proposed a Friday evenings only service for Forest Green, Oakwoodhill, Ockley and Holmbury St. Mary to Guildford, however permission for this was refused in April 1977 following objections from Tony McCann Motors, who themselves commenced a Friday evening service of route 845 on 3 June 1977.

Discussions also took place in early 1977 concerning the possibility of Tillingbourne operating an infrequent service from Billingshurst to Cranleigh, and even taking over the Alder Valley 269 service, whose deficit was causing West Sussex County Council some concern, however Surrey County Council expressed doubts over possible competition with Alder Valley service 283 between Nanhurst Corner and Guildford. The possibility of Tillingbourne operating the 269 route does not seem to have progressed any further, however in October 1977 Tillingbourne put a proposal to Surrey County Council to operate a revised 448 service timetable which cut the number of Cranleigh journeys but which incorporated route 452 by way of an extension to serve Billingshurst on Mondays to Fridays. However, while this

**60. Identical to GPA 846N in photograph 56, MPE 248P was delivered in April 1976. It currently works for East Surrey Buses, as indeed did GPA 846N before it. (N.Hamshere)**

**61. ACU 303C was new to Hall Bros., South Shields and was a 51 seat Leyland Leopard with Harrington body. It was often used by Tillingbourne on school contract work but here it is at Stourpaine Bushes Traction Engine Rally whilst performing a Private Hire. (MB Transport Photos)**

might have been acceptable to West Sussex County Council, it does not seem to have appealed to Surrey County Council, and nothing further was heard of it.

In the early summer of 1977, London Country, in co-ordination with Surrey County Council, introduced a specialist Sunday leisure service, route 417, which operated a clockwise route from Dorking to Coldharbour, Forest Green, Holmbury St. Mary, Abinger Common and Westcott and which was marketed as the "Ramblers Bus". In 1978, this successful service was re-routed to operate from Forest Green to Ewhurst, Peaslake, Gomshall and Abinger Hammer, before rejoining the existing route at Holmbury St. Mary. Not to be outdone, and with a need to operate additional mileage in order to fulfil new bus grant requirements, Tillingbourne introduced its own "Scenic Circular" service in May 1978 which operated from Guildford via Godalming, Busbridge, Winkworth Arboretum, Hascombe, Nanhurst Corner, Cranleigh, Ewhurst, Peaslake, Gomshall, Shere, Newlands Corner and Merrow. The service was sufficiently successful to be repeated in 1979 with an extension from Hascombe to Dunsfold and Alfold Crossways, however, again, once the novelty value had worn off the loadings were erratic. On several days, the service was saved from disastrously poor takings by a party of Dutch visitors who appeared unexpectedly at Coneyhurst Lane between Ewhurst and Peaslake where they were staying at a training establishment and who proceeded to have a thoroughly enjoyable tour around West Surrey! The service was not re-introduced for the 1980 season.

In 1977 Tillingbourne acquired a secondhand vehicle which fitted very well into the fleet, GGR 344 N, a Bedford YRQ with a Willowbrook bus body which had originated with Economic of Whitburn and was, in fact, exhibited at the 1974 Commercial Motor Show. Following the purchase of Economic by Tyne and Wear PTE, the Bedford was out of place in the new owners normal fleet and was consequently sold when only three years old. There were three new arrivals in the 1977/78 period, all Bedfords: SPA 192 R, a Bedford YMT with an attractive 53 seat Plaxton Supreme coach body, complete with "Bristol" dome; WPL 985 S, a Bedford YLQ with a Plaxton coach body which in most respects resembled LPE 42 P and XPL 889 T, a Bedford YMT with Duple Dominant 61 seat bus body. The latter vehicle was interesting for several reasons, firstly the choice of body was as a result of Plaxton withdrawing from the bus body market, secondly it was the forerunner of many similar vehicles of various different chassis types, and thirdly it set a trend by achieving high capacity through the use of three and two seating for the back half of the vehicle. This was initially required for operation of the 451 in Horsham, where the number of school children carried was considerable. Although sometimes criticised for the narrowness of the seats on such vehicles, Tillingbourne have always been convinced that this layout is preferable for rural routes to the standee type layout typified by the Leyland Nationals operated by the NBC companies. By this time, new buses joining the Tillingbourne fleet had a standard internal appearance, with bright yellow-based moquette covered seats and much use of wood grain laminates, which produced an impression of luxury far greater than the all-white interiors and pvc covered seats favoured by their larger neighbours. At the end of 1978, the Tillingbourne fleet was, for the first and last time, all-Bedford, totalling nine vehicles, eight of which had been purchased new,

**62. Bedford YRQ/Willowbrook bus GGR 344N has had six owners: Economic of Whitburn, Tyne & Wear P.T.E., Tillingbourne, McCann, Gastonia of Cranleigh and East Surrey Buses, for whom it still operates. The new Friary Centre in Guildford is seen under construction in the background. (Authors Collection)**

**63. With a similar body to LPE 42P, Bedford YLQ WPL 985S was in the fleet for five years from 1978. This private hire job to Hillingdon was driven by Peter Larking who was subsequently a director of Tillingbourne (Metropolitan) and now Metrobus Ltd. (G.Burnett)**

and with an average age of three years - a quite remarkable change of affairs in the six years since 1972.

In 1979 there were major changes to the Company's operations. A continued increase of new housing in the North Heath area of Horsham, together with the rural section of service 451 becoming increasingly unremunerative, led Tillingbourne to take a decisive step towards the conversion of the 451 into a local town service. A new timetable was introduced from 29 January which completely revised the service with the majority of journeys operating in a clockwise loop via Pondtail Road, Holbrook Corner and North Heath Lane. Interworked with these were four return journeys from Lambs Green and Rusper to Horsham via North Heath Lane, although the last return journey from Horsham terminated at Rusper. Somewhat surprisingly, all journeys retained route number 451. The afternoon journey to Warnham was withdrawn. The new timetable provided an approximately hourly service, although on an uneven headway, however it could still be operated by one vehicle and driver. As a result of these changes, the Tillingbourne Horsham network was now completely commercial and no subsidy was received from West Sussex County Council. In order to replace the service to Colgate, West Sussex County Council arranged for London Country to operate a new service, route 474, which operated between Horsham and East Grinstead, via Colgate, Pease Pottage, Crawley and then the 434 routeing. A year later, in January 1980, it was diverted to serve Faygate.

Over in the Guildford area there were also significant changes. Throughout the country, NBC companies were in the process of conducting "MAP" surveys which used computer projections of the results of completed questionnaires and loading data to produce revamped networks which were ostensibly for the benefit of the public, but which also optimised staff and vehicle resources to the mutual benefit of the operators and local authorities paying network revenue support. Such surveys were carried out in Guildford during 1979 and resulted in major changes the following year. Surrey was somewhat late to receive the effects of "MAP" however, and in other parts of England and Wales new marketing names were all the vogue to herald in the new networks. Possibly influenced by these events, Tillingbourne published a new timetable for the revisions commencing on 2 January 1979 which was entitled "PENDIBUS". This marketing name was intended to refer to the Company's indePENDance and dePENDability but, thankfully, the name did not appear on the vehicles and swiftly fell into disuse. Nevertheless, the message behind "PENDIBUS" was clear enough, and it is worth quoting from the leaflet itself, "At Tillingbourne we all have PSV driving licences and so garage and office staff can cover for drivers on holiday or off sick. This means that we don't suffer from buses being cancelled because there is no one to take them out. We don't clain to be infallible (we have the same delays due to traffic congestion etc. as everyone else) but when we tell you that this year we missed only 52 out of 160,259 scheduled bus miles - and this for all reasons - we think you will agree that's not a bad record."

The changes themselves included the extension of most journeys of service 448 through to Cranleigh to make a regular hourly frequency, the curtailment of service 452 to operate from Plaistow to Cranleigh except during school holidays when it continued to run from Wisborough Green, and a reduction in frequency of service 454 to once a month again, apart from during August, when it operated on every

**64. In order to cater for increased school traffic, a 61 seat bus was purchased for the Horsham 451 route in September 1978. XPL 889T was a Bedford YMT with Duple Dominant body and is depicted in the Carfax in Horsham. It was sold with the Orpington operations to Metrobus. (N.Hamshere)**

**65. A particular favourite with some was CPG 160T, a Plaxton-bodied AEC Reliance. In early 1987 it was photographed on the short-term West Sussex County Council contracted Horsham local service 292 after partial withdrawal by Southdown. The coach was acquired by Steven Salmon when he left Tillingbourne to set up his own Hedgerow Travel business, and is now operated as a driver training vehicle by London & Country. (R.J.Waterhouse)**

Wednesday. By this time, the Company was also beginning to advertise for private hire work having acquired a number of grant specification new coaches.

London Country, in conjunction with Surrey County Council, were anxious to extend route 412 (which operated from Sutton Abinger to Dorking via Holmbury St. Mary, Abinger Common and Westcott) to Cranleigh via Forest Green and Ewhurst. Despite objections from Tony McCann Motors, this was achieved as from 1 September 1979. McCann had planned a similar facility, although on a far more infrequent basis, and on 4 September 1979, he commenced a twice weekly (Tuesdays and Thursdays) service from Ockley to Cranleigh via Oakwoodhill and Walliswood, a service similar to that originally proposed by Tillingbourne in November 1976. Alder Valley were undoubtedly unhappy about the appearance of another operator on the Ewhurst to Cranleigh section of their service 273, however as the interloper this time was a fellow NBC company, it was reluctantly agreed that there would be no restrictions on picking up and setting down passengers on this section. This, in turn, caused the retention of such restrictions on Tillingbourne's service 448 to be indefensible, and they were withdrawn at the same time as the commencement of the 412 extension. The London Country service turned out to be far from successful, and the extension to Ewhurst and Cranleigh was withdrawn on 22 August 1981. However, by this time, Tillingbourne's service was an established part of Cranleigh's public transport facilities and thus there was no attempt to reapply any restrictions on the 448 route. Not surprisingly, McCann's service was altered on 3 December 1981 to start from Holmbury St. Mary, and then via Forest Green to Ockley in order to attract the limited number of passengers who had used the 412 service to Cranleigh.

The final change to Tillingbourne's bus services in 1979 came about from 24 September, and were perhaps the most significant. The 451 service in Horsham was doubled in frequency to make a regular half hourly service, leaving the Carfax at 15 and 45 minutes past the hour, except on Saturdays, when the service remained hourly. So successful was this development, that these times continued in operation right through the 1980s. On Mondays to Fridays a second vehicle was required to operate the schedule, and once again a bus was outstationed at the British Rail yard near Horsham Station. Perhaps the most interesting feature of these changes was that an additional journey was operated on the 451 on Mondays to Fridays, leaving the Carfax at 1845 hours, and, as the regular Tillingbourne driver could not legally perform this journey within his shift, it was arranged that it would be operated by London Country. This was achieved by using the layover time of a Leyland National operated 414 journey, and demonstrated that relations between the two companies were considerably better than they had been some years before. The service to Rusper and Lambs Green was maintained, but, logically, was renumbered 452, the Wisborough Green to Cranleigh Fridays only service being changed from 452 to 453 at the same time.

In the twelve months to December 1979, no less than four new vehicles were acquired, one being a Bedford CF Minibus to operate a school contract from the Leith Hill area to Dorking, and the new commitments brought the fleet strength up to eleven vehicles. The other new purchases were also of interest, being CPG 160 T, an AEC Reliance with Plaxton Supreme 53 seat coach body, EPH 27 V, a further Bedford YLQ but this time with Duple Dominant 52 seat bus body and finally JTM

109 V, another AEC Reliance but with Duple Dominant bus body. The AEC vehicles demonstrated Tillingbourne's wish to maintain a heavyweight chassis presence in the fleet and reinforced the Company's quandry that the Bedfords, despite their excellent service, were not quite man enough for some of the work required of them, while heavyweight chassis were overspecified for the Company's rural routes. In fact both AECs were to give excellent service, and were generally found to be superior to the equivalent Leylands from both the driving and the engineering points of view. Interestingly, CPG 160 T had a ZF 6 speed manual gearbox, which was quite a handful on bus work, whereas JTM 109 V had a 5 speed semi-automatic gearbox. In the pursuit of the ideal bus, Tillingbourne borrowed a Leyland National demonstrator and a Ford R type bus with the new inclined engine at different times. The Leyland National had a fully automatic transmission, and was popular with the drivers, but not with the management when it was discovered that the fuel consumption was almost twice that of the Bedfords. The Ford was generally regarded as inferior to the equivalent Bedford vehicles. Two vehicles were sold during 1979 to Tony McCann Motors, who were similarly disillusioned with Ford products, having had several ex-Midland Red units in their fleet, the vehicles involved being LPD 12 K and GGR 344 N. Thus at the end of the year, the whole fleet had been purchased new, and the average age was a remarkable two years.

**66. Conversely, Bedford YLQ EPH 27V had few supporters. It had 52 seat Duple bodywork with "3+2" seating at the rear. Seen at a temporary stand in the Onslow Street Bus Station, it was unique in having very large fleetname lettering. (P.R.Nuttall)**

67. AEC Reliance JTM 109V started its career on routes 448/450 in late 1979, was transferred to Orpington in 1981 and was then leased to Metrobus for three years from September 1983. However, it was returned early to Cranleigh in 1985 and is still in the fleet, having been refurbished in 1989. In this view it is on route 355 to Forestdale when with Tillingbourne (Metropolitan). (M.Dryhurst)

68. One of several Manufacturers' Demonstrators to be tried in service was COO 242T, a Ford R1014. At the wheel in Guildford in 1979 was Author George Burnett, who did not gain a particularly favourable impression of the vehicle. (MB Transport Photos)

However the Company still needed to resolve the problem of finding a truly suitable operating base, and this was causing over-riding difficulties in the late 1970s. Not only was the Ewhurst Garage considered by many local residents to be environmentally unacceptable, but a small garage built to accommodate 14 seater vehicles was totally unable to cope with the 11 metre vehicles now common in the Tillingbourne fleet, and these could only be serviced with the back doors left wide open with consequent noise and disturbance. The diesel pump which was positioned on the pavement was a very welcome additional facility for the Company, but regular visits by vehicles pulling up to be filled (sometimes even while in service) did not help to pacify the Company's neighbours. The site itself created difficulties for Tillingbourne, with vehicles constantly having to be shuttled between Ewhurst and Gomshall, and with an artificial limitation placed on the Company preventing the natural expansion in activities which were necessary for future financial health. In 1978, one local resident became so indignant that the Company was taken to Court for creating a private nuisance, and although the judge ruled that the Company was doing everything possible to minimise noise and smoke emission, the latter problems were still sufficient to justify issuing an injunction against the Company, although, fortunately, this was suspended for one year. After losing its appeal to the Secretary of State, the Company had been reluctant to apply for a temporary building extension, as suggested by the local authority, as it was felt that there would be little or no resultant financial return or guarantee of tenure.

Yet again the situation looked bleak, however in November 1978 Barry King wrote to Waverley District Council, having been informed by the Corporate Planning Officer of that authority that surplus council premises at Littlemead, Cranleigh were being offered for rent. The facilities concerned were ideal for the Company and would allow adequate parking for the entire fleet, maintenance facilities, office space, a mess room and toilets. Tillingbourne were very concerned that other parties were also interested in Littlemead, and thus the letter asked for special consideration to be given to the Company, in the light of the problems experienced during the previous seven years. Surrey County Council were also asked to endorse the Tillingbourne plea, which they did in March 1979, and after a protracted period the Company finally took possession of Littlemead at the end of 1980. However, in the meantime, 1980 itself was a very significant year for bus operations in the West Surrey area.

# CHAPTER 5 - WEYFARER AND PASTURES NEW

Mention has already been made of the National Bus Company inspired MAP schemes which were introduced all around England and Wales in the late 1970s and early 1980s. Alder Valley, whose finances were in a particularly poor state, was anxious that its entire operating area should benefit from thorough MAP examination. In the case of that Company's operations in the Woking and Guildford areas, it was necessary to obtain the active participation of not only the local co-ordinating authority, but also the neighbouring NBC subsidiary, London Country Bus Services, and the three independent bus companies, some of whose services ran jointly or in parallel with NBC ones. London Country, who never actually instigated an MAP scheme of their own, had already co-operated with Alder Valley in the Berkshire and Buckinghamshire areas where their services met, and thus agreed to participate again in the case of the Woking/ Guildford scheme. With the encouragement of Surrey County Council, Blue Saloon, Safeguard and Tillingbourne all co-operated in the MAP reviews, which proceeded apace throughout 1979 and the early part of 1980.

Tillingbourne recognised that the MAP scheme represented both a threat and an opportunity to the Company's ability to prosper and expand. Whilst the existing services were, in effect, thrown into the melting pot, the potential thinning out or even withdrawal of the larger companies' services could well present the opportunity for Tillingbourne to provide replacement facilities. In March 1980, Tillingbourne wrote to Surrey County Council with regard to discussions which were taking place between the Company and London Country and also to make certain suggestions regarding the Dunsfold/Hambledon area. The two companies were working on a new co-ordinated timetable for the services operating between Gomshall, Shere and Albury to and from Guildford which would enable both of them to make resource savings. As has been mentioned previously, Tillingbourne had been making extensive use of central government grant to assist in the purchase of new vehicles, however with the use of these funds came an obligation that a fixed percentage of each vehicle's mileage would be for stage carriage operation. Rationalisation with London Country would mean mileage savings which would have caused problems in this respect, and, consequently, Tillingbourne suggested to the County Council that the Company would be prepared to exchange one of its full sized vehicles for a 16 seater minibus which could be used to replace loss-making Alder Valley services in the Dunsfold and Hascombe areas. A schedule was suggested which maintained the normal Cranleigh to Godalming service, via Dunsfold, Hascombe and Busbridge, incorporated school and shopping journeys between Hambledon and Godalming via Hydestile and allowed for a limited number of journeys to operate direct from Hambledon to Dunsfold and Cranleigh. In the event, these suggestions were not taken up and Alder Valley continued to provide the service in these areas.

In the meantime, a further development in the Horsham area saw the Company introduce schooldays only journeys on service 451 between Kingsfold and Horsham via Northlands, Warnham and Holbrook Corner from March 1980 and in July that year, on Tuesdays and Fridays, the morning off-peak journey of service 452 from

Horsham to Lambs Green was advanced and extended to Crawley, with a similar return from Crawley three hours later.

**69. A matching twin for XPL 889T in photograph 64 came in the shape of CCG 550V. These two buses were regularly allocated to the Horsham outstation and virtually monopolised route 451 in the early 1980's. Here, CCG 550V was near Horsham Station on 6 September 1980. (E.C.Churchill)**

In line with the normal practice of providing local marketing names, the Woking/Guildford MAP scheme was dubbed "Weyfarer", and it was implemented with a considerable publicity effort as from 31 August 1980. As far as Tillingbourne was concerned, the changes were not too extensive, although they were certainly to the benefit of the overall profitability of the Company. No major re-routeings were involved, a small number of poorly used journeys were withdrawn, noticeably the 1830 hours departure from Guildford of service 448 which meant that the last departure of this service from Guildford was now at 1745 hours. However there was also a new peak hour service on 448, together with a reduction in journey time which resulted in the service offering a faster time between Ewhurst and Guildford than the main Alder Valley 273 route. Because of the introduction of an Alder Valley route 450 in the Aldershot/Camberley area within the "Weyfarer" network, the Farley Green service was renumbered from 450 to 445, and there were revised timings which provided an approximate half hourly service with London Country 425 between Albury and Guildford, which latter route was itself rationalised to an hourly frequency, with the 439 route no longer extending west from Dorking. For the first time return ticket inter-availability was introduced for London Country, McCann and Tillingbourne services operating between Gomshall/Shere and Albury to Guildford, by whichever route; for all services operating between Merrow and

Guildford, including Blue Saloon; for all services operating between Shalford and Guildford, and for Alder Valley and Tillingbourne services operating between Cranleigh and Ewhurst. Curiously, the latter did not include London Country's 412 service. Another sign of co-operation between the different operators was the introduction of the Guildford Travelwide scheme where, within the town limits, a pass could be used as many times as needed on any of the local operators' services; this scheme was to survive the upheavals of the following years until it was eventually discontinued in late 1988.

Tillingbourne also introduced a special return ticket available in the morning peak period, the success of which obliged other operators to follow suit later. This return ticket offer, which tied the user to a Tillingbourne vehicle for both journeys, together with a two week introductory free return journey offer for Surrey County Council Concessionary Bus Pass holders, indicated a deliberate attempt to gain for the Company a dominant position along the Valley road, where for so long the Company had only had a minority share. Other changes introduced as a result of "Weyfarer" were also of some interest. The 453 service was withdrawn, which was hardly surprising as the Alder Valley 269 route had been diverted to operate via Cranleigh in 1978, thus making the Tillingbourne service from Plaistow, Loxwood and Alfold to Cranleigh largely superfluous. The 454 service from Cranleigh to Chichester was transferred to London Country, who renumbered it as route 854. This latter transfer may have been in connection with the adjustments to the 425 timetable, as not only were such irregular services almost unknown to London Country, but Chichester was a long way from the Company's normal operating territory and must have posed some considerable difficulties in terms of route learning for the drivers. Although this route had been very productive for Tillingbourne, its novelty value was wearing off and loadings were in decline, a fact verified by London Country's ultimate withdrawal of 854 on 1 September 1982.

In the light of reductions in the section of Alder Valley's service 269 between Plaistow and Horsham, Tillingbourne introduced service 446, which operated on Fridays only between Dunsfold and Horsham via Durfold Wood, Plaistow, Ifold, Loxwood and Tismans Common. There were picking up and setting down restrictions between Tismans Common and Horsham to protect Alder Valley service 283. Earlier in August 1980, Tillingbourne had written to West Sussex County Council indicating displeasure at that county's support of an application by Southdown to provide a similar link between Plaistow and Horsham by reminding that County that such services were provided at commercial risk by Tillingbourne with no outside financial assistance. Whereas previously the two companies had little mutual contact, the continued expansion of activities by Tillingbourne (Sussex) must have been an irritation for Southdown, in fact at the time of the changes in the North Heath area, Southdown had put forward the view that they should be the operator to provide services in urban areas of Horsham as Tillingbourne only had experience in providing rural services.

At the end of August, London Country made alterations in the Dorking/Horsham area whereby the 414 service no longer ran to Horsham, being replaced by an extension of Greenline service 714 which meant that London Country were no longer in a position to cover the last journey of service 451 in Horsham, hence it was withdrawn.

Although the premises at Littlemead were not yet available for occupation, the Company was able to use the parking space and thus, from 1 September, the four buses required for the Guildford area services were operated from Littlemead.

1980 also marked the passing of a Transport Act which, among other things, removed the requirement to obtain licences for the operation of excursions and tours. Tillingbourne operated an experimental number of Sunday excursions during the autumn of 1980, and for the 1981 season there was a comprehensive programme commencing in April and running through to November. Such was the enthusiasm for this new activity for the Company that towards the end of 1980, a new Bedford YMT coach with Duple Dominant bodywork, NDV 44 W, was purchased and this was notable as the first full size vehicle bought new which was not to bus grant specification. Other new arrivals to the fleet in 1980 were a Bedford YMT bus, CCG 550 V, similar in most respects to XPL 889 T, and a second hand AEC Reliance bus with Plaxton Derwent dual purpose bodywork, UKX 150 J, from the fleet of Red Rover.

**70. After its purchase from Red Rover of Aylesbury, AEC Reliance UKX 150J was used on Guildford services before being transferred to Orpington in April 1981. Although the Plaxton Derwent body was a bus design, it contained coach seating. (J.Marsh)**

On 2 November 1980 the new Friary Bus Station was opened in Guildford and for the first time all bus services, both local and long-distance, were concentrated together at one location in the town.

With the resolution of the premises problem at last in sight, Tillingbourne firmly turned its attention to expansion and already, by the end of 1980, the fleet strength had risen to 13 vehicles with the Company determined to seize all opportunities to create a firmer base for its stage carriage operations. The propensity of Tillingbourne to act in an unexpected fashion was soon to cause the neighbouring

NBC subsidiaries to recognise the Company as a threat to parts of their operating territory which could not be ignored. Thus, typically, in November 1980, Tillingbourne applied for a Road Service Licence to operate a circular service by extending the 448 route from Cranleigh to Guildford via Shamley Green, Wonersh and Bramley on a limited stop basis. The reasoning behind this application was ostensibly to cater for a demand for a "fast" service between Cranleigh and Guildford not provided by Alder Valley, many of whose services deviated to such places as Smithwood Common or Nanhurst. Although no morning peak hour service was provided for in the timetable, the Company quoted the County Council's 1977/78 Report on the Cranleigh area which had claimed that such a service would be attractive and would generate additional patronage.

After months of work in designing and co-ordinating the "Weyfarer" network, both Alder Valley and Surrey County Council must have been completely taken aback by this application, coming as it did only two or three months after the start of the new services. Alder Valley wrote an indignant letter to the County Council claiming that the granting of such a service would be against the public interest, as it might ultimately cause other services in the area to need additional public funding. After considering the application in some depth, the County Council resolved that an objection should be lodged with the Traffic Commissioners and that the Council should be represented at the subsequent Hearing. As a result, the application was dropped by Tillingbourne, however, any satisfaction that this may have caused Alder Valley would have been limited if they had noticed the exact wording of the resolution, which stated that the objection be made, "...on the grounds not least that at this stage it is premature...". More was to be heard in the future concerning Tillingbourne's desire to operate on the "direct" route between Cranleigh and Guildford.

On 16 March 1981, effectively marking the completion of the move to Cranleigh, the Company's registered address was changed to that of the Littlemead premises, however, even before that date, the Company had expanded its operations in a most unusual and unexpected area.

For a number of years, Tillingbourne had used a small number of part time drivers, who normally worked on weekend bus duties, rail service replacement work or private hires. One such driver was Peter Larking, a local government officer by profession, who, from time to time, worked the Saturday Horsham local bus shift. Peter lived some distance away in the Orpington area, and for a number of years had been interested in the activities of the local independent operators around Croydon and Orpington, amongst whom, coincidentally, had been North Downs Rural Transport. By 1980, all these services had passed to the Orpington and District Omnibus Company, which was run by a Miss Normington.

By the end of 1980, Orpington and District were operating route 853, Croydon to Orpington, route 855, Croydon to Forestdale Estate in peak hours only, route 857, Croydon to Orpington via Forestdale Estate in the off-peak and route 858, Orpington and Biggin Hill. All these services were operated on Mondays to Fridays only, as all Saturday journeys had been withdrawn in July 1980, and the vehicles used were mostly rather elderly Leyland Atlantean double deckers. In early 1981 it became clear that the company was facing serious difficulties, the 858 service failing to reappear after the Christmas holiday due to lack of finances to purchase spare parts for the Ford A series minibus used, and although it reappeared for three days in late January, from 16 February the 853 and 857 were reduced to peak hours only, being abandoned four days later. The 855 to Forestdale had an off-peak timetable added on 23 February, but abruptly terminated after the morning peak on 27 February, signalling the end of O & D due to financial difficulties and related vehicle maintenance problems.

Watching these events closely, Peter Larking and his colleagues would very much have liked to set up their own rescue operation, however they had neither the time, the funds nor the experience. Nevertheless, they set about trying to convince Barry King and Trevor Brown of Tillingbourne that there was considerable potential in the operating territory of O & D, and that they would be very willing to assist Tillingbourne should the latter be prepared to commit resources to continue the Orpington services. Although Croydon and Orpington are a considerable distance from Tillingbourne's home territory, the Company, having carefully studied the situation, decided to send up a coach to run a Monday to Friday peak hour service on 855 from Monday 2 March 1981.

Initial use of this skeleton service was promising, and Tillingbourne was able to obtain London Bus Agreements from London Transport so that from 21 April the 855 was renumbered 355 and the 853/7 re-appeared as 353/357, running Monday to Friday peak hour services on 353/5 and all day Monday to Saturday on 357, the latter to an hourly frequency. It is significant that this new venture was in no way a takeover and no attempt took place to purchase any residual "goodwill" or the vehicles of O & D, none of which were in an acceptable condition in any case. Instead, in March 1981, Tillingbourne acquired two of the last AEC Reliances built, both with Duple Dominant 2 coach bodies to bus grant specification and understood to be a cancelled order which would have been the last two of London Country's RB class of Greenline coaches. The vehicles were certainly equipped with the heavier duty brake specification common to Greenline coaches, and they were registered as ODV 404/5 W and dispatched to Orpington for use on the newly acquired routes. Although retaining his full-time job, in his spare time Peter Larking provided local management expertise with his two colleagues, Gary Wood and Mark MacWilliam, both former London Country bus drivers, assisting with the administration in addition to driving. The operation was marketed as Tillingbourne (Greater London) with the address of Cornwall Drive, St. Pauls Cray where the vehicles were parked, after an initial period when a farm off Jail Lane, Biggin Hill was used. Two of the former O & D drivers also joined the Company. The two new vehicles, together with the other vehicles from the main Tillingbourne fleet, were returned to Cranleigh for maintenance purposes on a rota basis, although the Company shortly moved to a new operating base at Oak Farm Garage, Farnborough Hill, Green Street Green with much improved maintenance facilities and which had, in fact, been the previous base for O & D. It was a site used by several other operators and was rented by the individual companies from Botton Bros. Amusements.

Tillingbourne started a small excursion programme from the Orpington/-Forestdale/Croydon area in June 1981 and the following month all operations passed to the newly-formed Tillingbourne (Metropolitan) Ltd., amongst whose directors were Trevor Brown, Barry King, Peter Larking, Gary Wood and Mark

MacWilliam. Vehicles operated by the new Company (although, like the Sussex subsidiary, there was a degree of interchanging of vehicles) were the Bedford YMT coach, SPA 192 R, UKX 150 J (the AEC Reliance bus from Red Rover), the two coaches mentioned above and JTM 109 V, the AEC Reliance bus purchased new by the Company in 1979. By November 1981, the operation was on such a sound footing, with both loadings and revenue consistently improving, that more minor improvements could be made to the peak-hour timings and the off-peak terminus in Croydon was extended to the Fairfield Halls for the benefit of shoppers. Reliability, publicity and a smart "big company" image had all contributed to a network of services which were so well used that it seems amazing that London Transport had not considered them to be worth operating when the small companies had started them a few years earlier.

Meanwhile, in the Guildford area, the Company had not been idle, introducing an extensive programme of excursions picking up at Guildford, Cranleigh, Merrow, Shere, Gomshall, Shalford, Chilworth, Wonersh, Shamley Green, Ellens Green and Rudgwick, with most also serving Ewhurst and Peaslake. A special feature of Wednesday excursions was free travel on the appropriate bus service with guaranteed connections to the excursion coach. In March 1981, adverse public comment was made in the local press concerning the off-peak shopping facilities for the village of Puttenham which resulted from the 1980 Weyfarer MAP scheme. Tillingbourne wrote to Surrey County Council offering to supplement the Alder Valley 265 service with an additional mid-morning journey between Guildford and Puttenham, worked off stand time available on one of the Guildford bus shifts, however this offer was not taken up by the Council, who finally managed in June 1981 to arrange for Alder Valley to provide an appropriate additional journey to serve Puttenham.

Following the disposal of the bus garage at Ewhurst, an unusual arrangement occurred whereby it was intended for the building to be dismantled and taken to the Chalk Pits Museum at Amberley in West Sussex to be re-erected as a typical small bus shed of the 1920s. It is understood that, in the end, not much of the building was used, but certain parts, notably the doors, were and the replica can now be seen at the museum in the guise of a Southdown garage, housing a fine array of vintage buses and equipment.

In 1980 Tillingbourne had advised West Sussex County Council that, during 1981, the Company intended to introduce a so-called "commercial" service for the Lambs Green and Rusper areas, unless the Council wished to make a subsidy contribution in order to maintain the existing level of service. As no such subsidy was forthcoming, in June 1981 Tillingbourne introduced a number of changes to services in the Horsham area. Off-peak journeys on route 452 to Rusper and Lambs Green were withdrawn on Mondays, Wednesdays and Thursdays and the Rusper to Lambs Green section was withdrawn on Saturdays. However, at the same time, two new services were introduced, the 453 number was re-introduced for a Mondays, Wednesdays and Thursdays service from Horsham to Steyning via Southwater and the 454 (another resurrected number) which operated on Tuesdays from Ewhurst to Brighton, via Cranleigh, Ellens Green, Horsham, Southwater, Henfield, Small Dole, Edburton, Fulking and Pyecombe. This latter service partly replaced withdrawn Southdown facilities in West Sussex, although it attracted a protest from

**71. AEC Reliance/Duple Dominant ODV 404/5W were originally ordered by London Country for Green Line use but they ended up being purchased by Tillingbourne in March 1981 for immediate allocation to the new Orpington area network. Both still operate for Metrobus and ODV 405W was caught by the camera in Patcham in June 1983 working Coastlink route 350. (E.C.Churchill)**

**72. Seen at Guildford's Friary Bus Station on 30 April 1983 was SPT 647V, the first of two such Bedford YMT buses purchased from Gypsy Queen (Langley Park Motor Co.). (D.Jones)**

Alder Valley that it ran too closely to certain 283 journeys between Cranleigh and Horsham. By this time, Tillingbourne's propensity to devise seemingly innocuous timetables which succeeded in abstracting patronage from certain journeys operated by the NBC companies had become apparent to all the local traffic managers, however on this occasion the Company's plea that the 454 timings were built around connections with the 448 and 451 bus services was reluctantly accepted.

The 454 service also incorporated what appeared to be a very novel method of internal cross-subsidy, whereby an arrangement was reached with a local small brewery at Edburton to use the once a week service to deliver supplies of beer to one or two public houses on the part of the route which had been abandoned by Southdown. Naturally this was mentioned in the press release explaining the new service, and resulted in some superb publicity for the Company, although there is much doubt as to whether the beer delivery scheme continued for long after the initial run.

In August 1981, there were minor changes to the Guildford area timetables, including the withdrawal of the Blackheath diversion of route 445 on Saturdays, and the introduction of a new service, route 447, which offered a Thursdays only shopping facility from Guildford to Cranleigh via Shalford, Chilworth, Albury, Farley Green and Shamley Green. In November that year another attempt to link Tillingbourne's area of operation with Croydon took place with the introduction of service 444, which operated on Thursdays only from Cranleigh via Shamley Green, Wonersh, Bramley, Shalford, Chilworth, Albury, Shere, Gomshall, Abinger Hammer and Westcott and thence non-stop to Croydon. This service also enabled the Company to exchange vehicles with the Croydon/Orpington area operation for service and maintenance purposes, although it was shortlived, being withdrawn in February 1982.

It will be recalled that Tillingbourne would have favoured a bus which could combine the virtues of both the lightweight Bedfords and the heavyweight AECs and Leylands, and in 1981 it seemed possible that such a vehicle might be manufactured by the Hestair Dennis Company. Although four Dennis "G" type vehicles had been operated in the late 1920s and early 1930s, together with a Loline double decker which had been briefly owned in 1972, locally produced Dennis vehicles had never featured prominently in the Tillingbourne fleet, unlike other independents such as Yellow Bus or the foremost user of Dennis vehicles in the country, the Aldershot and District Traction Company. Consequently, it was something of a surprise when Tillingbourne placed an order for the new Lancet chassis straight off the drawing board in 1979. Hestair Dennis hoped to produce a chassis which would be heavier duty than the Bedford "Y" series, but retaining the economy of operation noted with Bedford vehicles. In reality, the new chassis was almost an updated Bristol LH, a vehicle which during its lifetime had typically suffered from lack of proper development by the parent Leyland organisation and was in the process of being phased out, despite its popularity with several NBC companies and a number of independents. Hestair Dennis were keen to offer the new chassis with a Perkins engine, however they bowed to customer preference and agreed to fit the Tillingbourne vehicle with the Leyland 401 engine, which, unlike the LH, was mated to a Detroit Diesel Allison fully automatic gearbox. During the long gestation period, the Tillingbourne engineering staff made several visits to the

Guildford factory and were able to offer advice on service and maintenance features which were incorporated into the design. Unfortunately, neither Duple (not at this time yet owned by Hestair) or Plaxton were able to offer a bus body for the new chassis, consequently the order was placed with Wadham Stringer for a 10 metre length version of their new Vanguard body design, and the completed bus, registered TTA 650 X, was delivered at the end of 1981, complete with 3 plus 2 seating giving a seated capacity of 52.

**73. The first of the new Dennis Lancet vehicles to be delivered to any operator was TTA 650X with Wadham Stringer Vanguard body. Owing to a contact within the local vehicle licensing office at Exeter, several Tillingbourne vehicles received Devon registrations at that time. (J.Marsh)**

Secondhand purchases during 1981 were from Maidstone Borough Council, who provided a Bedford YRT with Willowbrook bus body, and Langley Park Motors of County Durham, who supplied a two year old Bedford YMT with Duple Dominant bus body, which, apart from lacking three track number blinds, fitted into the fleet very well. During 1981, the Company sold GPA 846 N, a favourite Bedford YRQ, but, interestingly, it was to remain in the county of Surrey operating bus services for several years to come, firstly with Banstead Coaches and then, from 1986, with East Surrey Buses until 1988 when it was involved in an accident with a lorry and had to be written off for spare parts, to the great regret of its owner.

# CHAPTER 6 RURAL EXPANSION

It might have been reasonable to think that, after the activities which had taken place in 1980-1981, 1982 would have been a quiet year, however this was not to be the case, and expansion continued unabated.

Under the Weyfarer scheme of 1980, inter-availability of return tickets had been introduced between points which were served by more than one operator in the Guildford area, although initially this did not apply between Guildford and Ewhurst/Cranleigh with Alder Valley and Tillingbourne because of the very different routeings involved. In reality, failure of certain drivers to accept some tickets issued by other companies continued to cause difficulties, and Tillingbourne had to request Surrey County Council on several occasions to act as arbitrators in such disputes. Nevertheless, the management of both the NBC companies and the independent operators were keen to co-operate with each other, and in February 1982 a joint leaflet was issued by Alder Valley and Tillingbourne advertising the existence of special cheap day returns and weekly tickets from Ewhurst and Cranleigh to Guildford which were all available for use on either company's services.

November 1981, Barry King wrote to Surrey County Council referring again to the difficulties experienced with return ticket inter-availability along the Tillingbourne Valley road and suggested that this matter could be resolved by a joint takeover of routes 412 and 425 by Tillingbourne and McCanns, which it was claimed would save the County Council in excess of £20,000 per annum. Following a meeting with officers of the County Council, a further letter was sent to the County Council in January 1982 outlining in detail the type of timetable which Tillingbourne would be prepared to operate. Both the 425 and the 448 would have retained an hourly frequency, with the 445 reduced to a very limited service for the benefit of Farley Green. It was claimed that this could be achieved at no additional cost to the County Council, although the provision of evening, Sunday and occasional services to Ranmore would be the subject of a separate agreement for additional revenue support.

It was clear that Barry King hoped to include these changes with the major revisions planned for the Banstead area whereby London Country would be taking over further operations from London Transport at the behest of the County Council. During the late 1970s and 1980s, there were persistent rumours concerning the possible closure of London Country's Dorking Garage, and it may have been that this was part of the original thinking behind the Tillingbourne initiative. However, the proposals now put forward suggested that Dorking and Guildford Garages should take over some of Reigate and Leatherhead Garages' duties in the light of London Country's new commitments in the Banstead area. Tony McCann himself had recently suffered a flying accident, and some doubt was thrown on his long term intentions regarding the bus and coach business. Consequently, it was now suggested by Tillingbourne that the 412 service be retained by London Country and, as a further inducement to persuade them to transfer the 425 service, Tillingbourne would have been prepared to hand over a school run between Ockley and Dorking. The letter concluded by suggesting further discussions, including direct talks with

London Country, in the hope of agreeing the proposals and arranging a co-ordinated service between Westcott and Dorking, with a view to implementation in August/September 1982. These proposals were, of course, very radical, and whilst they were not rejected by Surrey County Council, considerable time and effort was necessary on the part of the Council to investigate their practicality, consequently nothing more was heard about them for some time.

The ambitious excursion programme offered in 1981 had not proved to be particularly successful, and was largely dropped for 1982 and the coach purchased for this work sold, although regular excursion trips to the south coast in the Summer were continued, using the bus services to feed in traffic. In contrast, the excursion programme operated in the Croydon/Orpington area proved very successful and was continued in an expanded form in 1982. From 1 May 1982 until 30 September of that year, a special Saturdays and Sundays "Coastlink" service, route 350, was introduced by Tillingbourne Metropolitan, operating from Ramsden Estate to Brighton via Orpington, Locks Bottom, Coney Hall, New Addington, Forestdale, Selsdon, Sanderstead, Purley and Coulsdon. This was to become a regular annual event for the Company and its successor, being expanded in 1983 to operate on Tuesdays and Thursdays during August as well. A useful shoppers' bus to Bromley, numbered 354, started on 4 May 1982 from Sanderstead, Selsdon, Forestdale and New Addington with one return journey Monday to Friday, and from 22 November it was diverted to serve Bourne Vale, breaking new ground.

With the Holmbury St.Mary to Cranleigh section of route 412 withdrawn, and with Tony McCann's intentions still not clear, Tillingbourne's focus of attention turned to the area between Ewhurst and Dorking. In May 1982, the Company submitted a proposal to operate a limited service between Cranleigh and Dorking via Ewhurst, Forest Green, Ockley, Capel and Holmwood, with intermediate short workings on a one-way loop from Dorking via Holmwood, Newdigate and Blackbrook. The proposal involved the use of an existing school contract vehicle but, apart from the expected objections from London Country, it was met with a total lack of enthusiasm from Surrey County Council, who could see little point in the service other than an abstraction of revenue from the London Country services in the Holmwood, Capel and Newdigate areas. As an example, the Council cited the shopping time allowed for in Cranleigh, which would have been in excess of four hours, and it was felt that, if spare off-peak capacity was available, it could be put to much better use than this proposed timetable. Consequently, nothing further was heard about the service between Cranleigh and Dorking until later in the year, when a more modest facility was introduced.

It can now be seen that Tillingbourne was firmly intent on expanding their stage carriage operations in the Guildford area, and, with no further news concerning the proposed takeover of route 425, from 5 July 1982, route 447 was withdrawn and Guildford to Albury journeys of service 445 were extended to Shere, thus further strengthening the Company's position in the Tillingbourne Valley, despite objections from London Country. These new journeys from Shere usually connected with the 448 service from Cranleigh and Peaslake, thus allowing through facilities for journeys such as Peaslake to Chilworth etc. At the same time, the journeys to Farley Green were retimed and slightly reduced as patronage continued to decline from that village. The diversion of route 445 to serve Blackheath was reduced to a Thursdays only facility, and certain early and late journeys of route 448 were extended from the centre of Cranleigh to the Company's garage at Littlemead. The 446 service was also withdrawn, and replaced by a revised version of route 454. On Fridays, the service started from Cranleigh and then operated via Alfold Crossways, Alfold to Plaistow, where it turned round and continued to Horsham as the 446 had done, but operating direct from Loxwood to Tismans Common. On Tuesdays, the service started from Albury (except in school holidays, when it commenced at Gomshall and operated via Shere) and continued to Cranleigh via Chilworth, Wonersh and Shamley Green and thence to Horsham via the same routeing as the Friday service, continuing to Brighton as previously. Service 453 was changed to operate on Tuesdays only, being worked by the 454 bus returning from Brighton at 1115 hrs and continuing beyond Horsham to Alfold Crossways on the 454 routeing, returning to Brighton as a 453 in time to work the 1545 hrs journey from Brighton of service 454.

**74. Generally regarded as a good-looking vehicle was TPL 762X, a Leyland Tiger with Plaxton Supreme V body, featuring a "Bristol" dome. However, it had the same 0680 engine as fitted to the Leyland Leopard, and performed with usual Leopard sluggishness! (P.R.Nuttall)**

In the North Heath area of Horsham, work on building the new housing estate was almost complete and Tillingbourne introduced a revised timetable and routeing for service 451 intended to provide better penetration of the estate. Although this proposal had always been made clear to both the local authority and the developers, indeed the estate spinal road had been designed and constructed with bus operation in mind, the announcement that the new service was to commence was greeted by some vociferous protests from certain new residents of the estate. Such was the furore that a Traffic Court Hearing was called, but it transpired that more residents were in favour of the new routeing than were against, and with the evidence that the new road had been purpose designed for bus operation, the Company won the day and the new service commenced on 5 July 1982. The route operated on a one way loop from North Heath Lane, via Coltsfoot Drive, Jackdaw Lane, Brook Street, Brook Road, Rusper Road, Giblets Lane and back to North Heath Lane, however this left Pondtail Road unserved by the 451, consequently most journeys of service 452 were diverted via Pondtail Road and some anti-clockwise workings out via North Heath Lane and returning via Pondtail were introduced. At the same time, the extension to Crawley was reduced to operate on Fridays only, and the entire service was withdrawn on Saturdays.

From 6 September, another new service was introduced on Fridays only between Cranleigh and Arundel via Alfold, Loxwood, Adversane, Pulborough, Bury and Amberley, numbered 455. Whilst laying over in Arundel, the bus performed a short return journey to Burpham as service 456, both routes being an attempt to provide replacement services for further Southdown withdrawals. As from the same date, the Fridays journeys of route 454 commenced from Alfold Crossways instead of Cranleigh.

No sooner had the above changes in the Guildford and Horsham areas been implemented in July, than Barry King wrote once more to Surrey County Council concerning the possible takeover of the 425 service. This time, a scheme had been worked out which would enable Dorking Garage to be closed, and which entailed joint operation by Tillingbourne, McCanns and an unnamed coach operator in the Dorking area, who, it was claimed, was prepared to become involved in bus operation. At this time, Surrey County Council was coming under increased budgetary pressure, and the 425 route was one of the highest cost supported services in the county. The Tillingbourne scheme was carefully worked out to demonstrate how no less than five peak vehicles could be saved, and involved transfer of route 414 (Dorking to Croydon via Brockham, Reigate, Redhill, Merstham, Coulsdon and Purley) to Reigate Garage, transfer of Greenline route 714 to Leatherhead Garage (or even by joint operation with Southdown), and the transfer in amended form of routes 412, 425, 439 and 449 to the independent companies. Fully worked up draft timetables were enclosed, and although not stated specifically, it would appear that Tillingbourne would takeover the 425, the Dorking operator the 439 and 449 (that is the services from Dorking to Goodwyns Estate, Chart Downs Estate, Brockham, Leigh and Newdigate) and McCanns the 412 and the new 445/845, which was envisaged as a combination of Tillingbourne 445 and McCanns 845 and 852 routes from Guildford to Horsham via Chilworth, Shere, Holmbury St.Mary, Forest Green, Walliswood and Warnham, with short workings operating via Farley Green. This latter proposal may have been made with the strong possibility of a transfer of McCanns bus operations to Tillingbourne following confidential negotiations between the two operators concerning the possible sale of McCann's business. The proposals for the Cranleigh to Dorking service were still under consideration at that time, and a meeting was arranged between Tillingbourne, London Country and Surrey County Council for the 15 September 1982.

By the time that this meeting took place, negotiations between Tillingbourne and Tony McCann were complete for the transfer of all the McCann bus services to

Tillingbourne as from 1 November 1982. Also included in the agreement were three of McCann's vehicles, although no transfer of property or premises were to take place, McCann retaining a number of vehicles for contract and private hire purposes with an agreement not to re-enter local bus operation in competition with Tillingbourne. With the extensive service revisions necessary for the takeover, together with Surrey County Council's cautious approach to the radical proposals for the Dorking area and London Country's hostility, the meeting on 15 September merely seems to have resulted in all parties endorsing the new services planned following the integration of the McCann routes, and agreeing to the introduction of a limited facility to be operated between Cranleigh and Dorking by Tillingbourne as route 444, using vehicles employed on school contract duties. The routeings agreed no longer included Capel, Newdigate and Holmwood, although there was a Thursdays only return journey from Ockley to Cranleigh via Oakwoodhill, Walliswood, Forest Green and Ewhurst Green, which replaced McCann's route 846. No replacement was provided for McCann's route 844, which operated on Fridays only between Forest Green and Dorking via Leith Hill and Coldharbour, as the Post Bus service was now allowed to carry passengers on that day as well as on Mondays to Thursdays. McCann's routes 845 and 852 (Forest Green to Guildford via Holmbury St.Mary, Abinger Hammer, Gomshall, Shere, Albury and Chilworth and Forest Green to Horsham, via Ewhurst, Walliswood, Oakwoodhill, Ockley/Rowhook, Warnham and Broadbridge Heath) were combined into a new route 446, which incorporated many new through and connectional facilities and, for the first time ever, a journey from Forest Green, Holmbury St.Mary and Sutton which arrived in Guildford before 0900 hours for work and educational purposes. The 446 also connected with the 448 route at Ewhurst, permitting such journeys as Peaslake to Horsham, together with early morning and early evening peak journeys from Cranleigh to Horsham and return. Logically, the workings of service 445 between Shere and Guildford were renumbered as 446, with only the Farley Green journeys retaining the 445 number. Finally, a new Tuesdays only service, route 457, was commenced from Cranleigh to Brighton, via Ewhurst, Forest Green, Walliswood, Oakwoodhill, Ockley, Warnham and Horsham; this ran only during school holidays.

There was considerable interest in the vehicles purchased during 1982. Since the sale of the Dennis Loline, which was briefly owned in 1972, no double deckers had been operated by the Company, partly because of their unsuitability on Tillingbourne's rural routes, partly because there were no suitable servicing facilities for that type of vehicle, and partly because only a few of the drivers possessed licences to drive double deck buses. Prior to purchasing large capacity single deckers for the Horsham area, the Company had considered buying a double decker to cope with school movements there, however the factors previously mentioned, together with the low bridge in Pondtail Road meant the abandonment of the idea. Tillingbourne was approached by Safeway Supermarkets, who were prepared to pay for an overall advertisement bus which would serve the Forestdale Estate, however they were insistent that only a double decker bus would be suitable. The Oak Farm Garage was better able to deal with the maintenance of such a vehicle, many of the drivers were suitably licenced from O & D and London Country experience and the financial equation was attractive, particularly with the ever

**75. XTT 5X was the second Dennis Lancet and arrived in June 1982. It was driven in service by Stephen Morris, Editor of "Buses" magazine as part of a Test Drive and he is seen taking it across the bridge over the River Tillingbourne by Gomshall Mill on service 448. (A.Burney)**

**76. The only vehicle acquired with the McCann bus routes which was retained was NMJ 279V, a Bedford YMT/Plaxton, the only vehicle purchased new by McCann. (P.R.Nuttall)**

increasing loads experienced, which often led to certain key peak hour journeys being conductor operated. The only restraining factor was the low bridge in Coombe Road, Croydon which restricted the vehicle height to 13' 6". Consequently, in March 1982 Tillingbourne made the surprise purchase of a former West Yorkshire Road Car Bristol VRT double decker, BYG 851 H, which was promptly painted into Safeway advertising livery and entered service with the Metropolitan subsidiary.

Two interesting new purchases were that of TPL 762 X, a hybrid Leyland vehicle with a smart Plaxton Supreme V coach body and XTT 5 X, a second Dennis Lancet with Wadham Stringer bodywork, but this time with conventional manual gearbox. The Leyland vehicle was an experimental Tiger chassis, but equipped with a Leopard engine and gearbox and generally behaved and felt more like a Leopard than a Tiger. The Company was still not entirely convinced about the virtues of fully automatic gearboxes on their rural routes, hence the choice of manual change in the second Lancet, however this was an experimental fitment by Hestair Dennis using a cable change, and, as far as is known, was unique among Lancet chassis. In later days this bus was not universally popular with drivers, but was always a firm favourite of Barry King, who could usually be seen behind its wheel on Saturdays. A further secondhand Bedford arrived from Langley Park Motors and a diesel engined Ford Transit with Dormobile/Yeates converted standard coachwork replaced the petrol engined Bedford CF. The three vehicles purchased from Tony McCann Motors were LPD 12 K, the former Tillingbourne Bedford YRQ, which was in very poor mechanical condition and was dispatched to Yeates, the coach and bus dealers, on the 31st of October 1982, the day after the last day of McCann's bus operation, KAP 20 L, a Bedford YRT coach which was used as a spare vehicle for several months before being sold back to Tony McCann, and NMJ 279 V, the only vehicle ever purchased new by McCann, which was a bus grant specification Bedford YMT with Plaxton Supreme coach bodywork, similar to several such vehicles in the Tillingbourne fleet. With all the new commitments, it was not surprising that the fleet strength had risen from nine vehicles at the beginning of 1979, to nineteen vehicles at the end of 1982, although the average age remained a remarkable three years.

Within the triangle created by the towns of Guildford, Dorking and Horsham, Tillingbourne was now by far the most dominant operator, however, of the main routes connecting the three towns, the Company had made little impact on any, except for between Guildford and Abinger Hammer. Efforts to takeover the Guildford to Dorking route had been forestalled, the attempt in 1980 to obtain a share in the main route between Guildford and Cranleigh had been blocked by Alder Valley, and the recent attempt to operate on the Capel to Dorking road had been withdrawn following objections from London Country. The Company had achieved remarkable profitability considering the unremunerative nature of its routes, however it was well aware that a sounder revenue base would become essential to achieve continued financial success. Useful though the former McCann routes were, the result was a diversion of additional resources into areas of only marginal profitability, whereas success in gaining footholds on the main routes described above would have led to substantially better returns on the capital invested in buses and the additional staff costs.

# CHAPTER 7 - GETTING INTO SHAPE

Following the hectic events of the previous three years, 1983 was largely a year of consolidation and retrenchment as far as Tillingbourne's bus services in the Guildford and Horsham areas were concerned. However, it was also one where the seeds were sown for the future advancement of the Company by means of acquiring more profitable bus services in the district.

It had soon become apparent that some of the Tillingbourne off-peak experimental services started in 1982, together with elements of the former McCann network of routes, were distinctly unprofitable. Therefore, from 28 February 1983, the Thursdays only journeys of route 444 between Ockley and Cranleigh, and the 455, 456 and 457 routes were all withdrawn, to be followed in May by route 453.

In the meantime, the need for Surrey County Council to make significant reductions to their revenue support budget continued, in fact it became apparent that the Council would need to make a saving for the 1983/84 Financial Year in the region of £500,000. Naturally, in these circumstances, schemes which had not seemed either to require urgent action or to be particularly attractive, were given far closer inspection. In March 1983, Tillingbourne again wrote to the County Council, this time to respond to requests from the Authority to produce some rather drastic schedules which incorporated the total withdrawal of route 425 (with the 448 being diverted from Shere to operate via Albury, Chilworth and Shalford to Guildford), and with the addition of an evening service to replace that provided by the 425 between Guildford and Gomshall. The proposals also reduced the 446 service by diversion of a limited number of 448 journeys from Ewhurst to operate via Forest Green, Holmbury St.Mary and Abinger Hammer, before rejoining the main route at Gomshall. In addition to the cost savings inherent in the withdrawal of the 425, Tillingbourne suggested that their own revenue support grant, which was to be £35,000 in 1983/84, could be negotiated downward and the Company also expressed interest in the takeover of route 412 and services operated by Alder Valley in the Alfold/Dunsfold area. A through service between Guildford and Dorking would have been retained by the 762 route, which was jointly operated by Alder Valley, Southdown and London Country between Reading and Brighton and which had commenced in 1982, following a Traffic Court Hearing where its introduction had been opposed by both British Rail and Surrey County Council.

The County Council obviously had second thoughts about the swift implementation of such drastic revisions, because in May 1983 the Authority wrote to Tillingbourne to say that it seemed unlikely that any further progress on the lines mentioned above would take place prior to 1984, following reassessment of the revenue support position on London Country and the "need to investigate further certain aspects of the service pattern west from Dorking". It was felt that it would be unwise to initiate short term changes in view of the more fundamental changes which might be necessary in the future, however there was no objection to Tillingbourne making minor revisions to the existing services. The County Council had decided how it intended to achieve the savings required, and their proposals would be published for consultation purposes later that month, with a view to implementation before March 1984, and the 425 changes would not form part of this exercise.

Barry King undoubtedly saw that, at last, positive opportunities were now a distinct possibility, however three courses of action were necessary in the immediate future, firstly to make a series of changes to the existing network in order to enhance profitability and generally "tighten up" the services following the McCann takeover. Secondly, it was necessary to resolve certain difficulties which it was considered existed with the Croydon/Orpington operation and with certain non-PSV companies owned by Trevor Brown and which affected the Tillingbourne group of companies. Thirdly, to devote considerable time to developing a strategy to ensure the expansion of bus services in the Guildford/Horsham areas. With the expansion which had already taken place over the last three years, combining these planning activities with the day to day management requirements of the Company was becoming somewhat difficult, thus some form of assistance was helpful, and it was at this stage that George Burnett, co-author of this book, obtained the position of Traffic Manager with the Company.

In pursuit of the first of these objectives, a number of significant changes were implemented as from June 1983. Loadings on the 446 route, which combined two former McCann services, were very poor from the Forest Green area, and variable, to say the least, from the Holmbury St.Mary, Walliswood and Oakwoodhill areas, consequently a large part of the mileage in the middle of the 446 service was unremunerative. From June, the 446 route was altered to operate between Guildford and Forest Green only, with some journeys terminating at Holmbury and retaining the Guildford to Shere short workings. The service between Cranleigh and Horsham, previously worked as a variation of route 446, was renumbered 450. Peak hour journeys were retained, however the off-peak facilities for Walliswood, Oakwoodhill, Ockley and Rowhook were reduced to Tuesdays, Fridays and Saturdays only, with Forest Green losing its service to Horsham, except on Saturdays. The through operation from Guildford to Horsham was retained on a limited basis on Saturdays, with the vehicles changing their blind display from 446 to 450, or vice versa, between Walliswood and Forest Green. Interestingly, the previous practice on Saturdays of drivers changing vehicles at Abinger Hammer on through journeys also ceased with the implementation of these changes. As the shifts were arranged for these through journeys to incorporate operation of journeys on the Horsham local service, 451, residents of North Heath Lane were offered the opportunity of a through Saturday morning shopping service to Guildford.

In the Horsham area itself, the 452 service was restricted to peak hour journeys and the Tuesday and Friday shopping facility for Lambs Green and Rusper, with the once a week Crawley operation withdrawn, and with all journeys operating via North Heath Lane instead of Pondtail Road. To complement the various journeys of service 450 described above, a number of short working circular variations of route 450 were introduced on Mondays to Fridays running between Horsham and Warnham, in one direction via Broadbridge Heath, and in the other via Pondtail Road and Warnham Station. Schoolday journeys no longer had to work a clockwise loop from Warnham up to Kingsfold and back via Northlands as the children involved were transferred to a school contract. However, the 450 service was extended to Tanbridge House School and carried a large number of children thence from Warnham, Warnham Station and North Heath.

Other minor changes introduced at this time were the introduction of a Thursdays shopping service from Ockley to Guildford, via Oakwoodhill and Walliswood, which, curiously, was classified as a variation of route 450 (it connected with the 446 service at Forest Green), and the Tuesdays 454 service to Brighton was extended to Worthing and started from Chilworth on Schooldays and Cranleigh on Non-Schooldays. In December that year, the 454 was also diverted to serve the village of Littleworth.

**77. The first example of the Plaxton Bustler body in the fleet was on Bedford YMT FOD 941Y, seen in Horsham's Wimblehurst Park Estate in February 1984. (E.C.Churchill)**

Mention has been made previously concerning Alder Valley's 269 route, which, by 1983, operated primarily between Plaistow and Guildford via Loxwood, Alfold, Cranleigh, Nanhurst Corner and Bramley, however there also remained a peak hour journey from Plaistow to Horsham, via Loxwood, Tismans Common, Bucks Green and then the 283 routeing. Alder Valley announced that this journey would be withdrawn from the beginning of the Autumn Term, and, as Tillingbourne could interwork this requirement with an existing Capel to Dorking school contract, the Company liaised with West Sussex County Council to introduce a replacement facility from 5 September. The new service started from Loxwood, and was used by a small number of workers and those attending Collyers Sixth Form College in Horsham. While the 446 service in the morning peak had been routed via

Broadbridge Heath, it had been noted that a large number of passengers were carried from there, as the service was scheduled to arrive some time before the Southdown service. With the introduction of the 450 route, the peak service no longer operated via Broadbridge Heath, and the introduction of the 454 enabled the Company to regain the lost custom, which was well worth catering for, as in West Sussex children were obliged to pay full fares prior to 0900 hours. Thus the morning journey was also operated on Non-Schooldays, and on Saturdays from Bucks Green only, although a reprimand awaited any driver who ran late and missed the revenue! The first week of operation was complicated by Alder Valley's Licencing Department failing to obtain permission from the Traffic Commissioners to withdraw the service in time, consequently three buses arrived at Broadbridge Heath within a five minute period, and tempers became frayed with certain Alder Valley staff, who did not realise that they were not supposed to be there at all!

Three new buses entered service during 1983, which were of considerable interest. Early in the New Year, MPE 248 P, the second of the pair of Plaxton Derwent bodied Bedford YRQ buses, was sold to Farnham Coaches, eventually joining the fleet of East Surrey Buses in 1988 as GPA 846 N had done before it. However, in March, Tillingbourne took delivery of a Bedford YMT with the new Plaxton Bustler bodywork, FOD 941 Y, which marked the return of Plaxton to building single deck bus bodywork. By this time, all Bedford "Y" series were fitted with turbocharged engines, although the bus version was less powerful than that fitted to coach chassis, nevertheless the new bus proved to be both well built and to have a lively performance, the main criticism being the excessive step height of the entrance. Tillingbourne's livery had remained unchanged since the introduction of the blue, yellow and grey scheme in 1972, although the application of the fleetname style was changed for new vehicles from the Dennis Lancet, TTA 650 X, to an attractive upright typeface of more "old fashioned" appearance. For some reason, the AEC Reliance, JTM 109 V, had the same typeface as its contemporaries, but applied in an upright style instead of being slanted. The new Bedford, FOD 941 Y, was delivered with a very wide yellow band, which continued around the front of the vehicle, with a correspondingly reduced application of Danube blue, and very large fleetnames were displayed at the front and on the sides in blue on the yellow background, as opposed to the previous style of white on the blue background.

The two new Dennis vehicles were proving to be quite acceptable, however the Company had now decided that it would not be purchasing any further new 10 metre buses, even allowing for the increased capacity of the three plus two seating. Whilst the new turbocharged Bedfords seemed adequate for the Guildford and Horsham areas, a heavier duty 11 metre bus specification vehicle was felt to be necessary for the Metropolitan fleet. Hestair Dennis had been developing an 11 metre version of the Lancet chassis, which it was originally intended to call the Lance. In the event, the technical specification was so different to the Lancet that the decision was taken to call the chassis the Dorchester, as it was equipped with air suspension, Gardner engines and Voith fully automatic transmission complete with built in retarder. In 1982, Tillingbourne ordered two such buses for the Croydon/Orpington operation, again fitted with Wadham Stringer Vanguard bodywork and three plus two seating. These vehicles were delivered in July 1983 and registered FOD 942/3 Y, and for the first few weeks of operation, it was intended to work them from Cranleigh, being close to the factory at Guildford should there prove to be any technical problems. Unfortunately, this was indeed the case, teething problems included air suspended drivers seats which catapulted the driver out of his seat when the bus hit a bump, overfilling of the header water tank, which was mounted behind the driver and on a few occasions led to the vehicle having to be exchanged with the driver suffering from heat exhaustion, and, most seriously, a number of drive belt failures which resulted in, either buses losing alternator charge, or compressor failures, which resulted in the loss of air pressure and consequential seized brakes. These problems were all eventually overcome, following liaison between Hestair Dennis and Gardner, and the vehicles were to give excellent service, although the driving staff tended to either love them or hate them. In any event, by the time they were operating reliably, the situation had changed with the Metropolitan subsidiary, and they were never to see service in the Croydon/Orpington area.

Undoubtedly the most unusual purchase at that time was that of a 1954 vintage Albion Victor FT39AN with a Reading of Portsmouth 36 seat bus body, which had previously been operated by Watson's Greys of St.Martins, Guernsey. Although it was always intended that this bus should work for its living, it was most unlikely that it would ever cover its purchase and maintenance costs, and thus it can be regarded as something of a sentimental acquisition. This bus remained in full Watson's livery of grey with a black roof, complete with Guernsey blind display, however it had been reregistered by its previous owner, when brought to the mainland, as 898 FUF. A new service, operated as route 446, was registered for Sundays and Bank Holidays to run between Guildford and Gomshall via the 425 routeing, offering two return journeys, and the Albion commenced the operation of this route on 10 July 1983. A special brochure was produced for the occasion and the route was marketed as the "Summer Vintage Bus Service", operating until the last Sunday in September. The service was advertised as a tourist attraction and the brochure, which was largely self financing through advertising revenue, was distributed widely. The timings allowed for an afternoon stop at Silent Pool, with a guided tour by the driver, and details of a four mile walk from Gomshall were available on the bus with an offer for the driver to conduct this tour, subject to weather permitting. The launch consisted of taking members of the press for an evening drive to the Black Horse at Gomshall, while on the return to Guildford, the local radio station interviewed the driver, who happened to be the Traffic Manager, to the accompaniment of authentic engine sounds and the clashing of teeth on the crash gearbox! Like the Scenic Circular before it, the service enjoyed only spasmodic success, the most notable day for passenger loadings being the August Bank Holiday, when the route was extended to Peaslake for the annual Village Fair. After September, the vehicle was put into storage and eventually sold, much to the relief of the Chief Engineer.

By early 1983, the success of the Metropolitan operation was becoming something of a managerial problem for Tillingbourne. The distances involved meant that day to day management had to be left to the local team in Orpington and, quite naturally, divergence of opinions occurred. One example of this was the part to be played in the operation by private hire and excursions. Since 1972, Tillingbourne had firmly put bus services as the highest priority, with all other activities very much subordinate to this, the less than successful excursion programme in 1980/81 having largely reinforced this view. The local directors of the Metropolitan operation, however, felt that circumstances were very different in their area, and that a thriving and extensive private hire and excursion business could be developed without any threat to the efficiency and profitability of the bus services. Matters progressed to the point where it seemed to the Cranleigh based directors that, either their own nominee should be appointed to manage the Metropolitan business to their instructions, or a looser form of association should develop, with the possibility of a management buyout or straight sale of the Company.

**78. The two Wadham Stringer- bodied Dennis Dorchesters originally intended for Orpington are pictured together at Littlemead Depot, Cranleigh after delivery in Summer 1983. (G.Burnett)**

When this situation was discussed with Peter Larking and Gary Wood (Mark MacWilliam having already left the Company, and his shares sold to the Cranleigh directors), they were immediately keen to gain full control of the business from Tillingbourne (Metropolitan) Ltd. Negotiations eventually led to a positive conclusion, with the last day of operation for Tillingbourne (Metropolitan) being 23 September 1983. The goodwill of the business was purchased for a very substantial sum considering that two years previously it had been worth nothing. The new company, Metrobus Ltd., took over the lease for the premises from Tillingbourne, and purchased two Tillingbourne Bedford vehicles, SPA 192 R a coach, and XPL 889 T, the first of the 61 seat buses, together with the Bristol VRT double decker, which by now was delicensed and in need of considerable maintenance expenditure. In addition, Metrobus leased, initially for a three year period, the three AEC Reliance vehicles which had initially been sent to Orpington, JTM 109 V and ODV 404/5 W. The Cranleigh Traffic Manager assisted at Orpington for the last week of Tillingbourne operation, and Metrobus commenced operation on 24 September with a new livery variation, achieved by painting the grey roof of XPL 889 T blue. Metrobus and Tillingbourne continued to enjoy an amicable working relationship which has lasted right up to the present time, although Metrobus itself, interestingly, has successfully expanded the local bus services side of the business almost out of recognition through winning several London Regional Transport contract bus services which require a substantial number of double deck vehicles.

Trevor Brown owned a petrol filling station in Basingstoke known as Eastlands Garage, together with various other enterprises. By mid 1983, the only business trading there was Eastlands Garage Ltd., half the premises having been sublet to a car rental company, and, due to changing circumstances, the petrol sales had fallen to the point where the business was no longer profitable, with Tillingbourne management having to concern themselves with its day to day operation. A number of changes were implemented to ensure that the business no longer lost money, however it was decided that, in order to integrate activities further, the Garage business should be transferred to Tillingbourne (Metropolitan) Ltd., with the Traffic Manager from Cranleigh directly supervising the local manageress. Following the sale to Metrobus, the Metropolitan Company remained in existence, with one operating licence being used on a Cranleigh based vehicle. In this way, the Company was transformed from a bus operator in Orpington to a petrol retailer in Basingstoke within the space of a few months!

With these problems resolved, or at least under control, the Cranleigh management could now turn their full attention to the matter of expanding local bus operation in the Guildford/Horsham area, this time by means of a concerted and wide ranging set of proposals together with the backing of the not insubstantial cash assets accrued from several years of successful trading and the sale of the Croydon/Orpington services to Metrobus.

Local Authorities had consistently found their role as co-ordinaters to be a difficult one throughout the 1970s and early 1980s. Caught up in a spiral of escalating operating costs and a continuous decline in the usage of public transport, most found it difficult enough to maintain existing networks, let alone be in a position to fund significant innovations and improvements. The National Bus Company and the Local Authorities had agreed a standardised method of presenting the costs of providing individual bus services, and, presented with these statistics, Local Authorities were able to see, not only which routes were the most expensive to subsidise, but also which had the lowest ratio of revenue to costs, a simple method of judging value for money. What Local Authorities had little control over, of course, was the operating costs of the various bus companies, and thus how efficient they were in the provision of local bus services.

Because of significantly high operating costs, and thus subsidy requirements, of London Transport in the late 1970s and early 1980s, Surrey County Council had pursued a steady and deliberate policy of trying to replace LT services by those of London Country, with the intention of effecting cost savings without significantly reducing service levels. A natural extension of this policy would have been to transfer the most costly NBC routes to independent operators with lower operating costs, however, with a few limited exceptions, this had not happened in Surrey. The reasons for this are complex, and largely revolve around the relationship between the NBC subsidiaries and the County Council and arguments involving the principle of cross-subsidy. If a route requiring a high subsidy were to pass from one operator to another with lower operating costs, there would undoubtedly be a reduction in the subsidy paid for that specific route, however, under the financial formula described above, the fixed costs and part of the semi-variable costs associated with that route would be re-distributed over the remaining routes operated by thecompany concerned. The result would be an increase in overall subsidy required for the remaining routes which could cancel out the saving in subsidy achieved by the original route transfer. In addition, when threatened by such a transfer, a bus company was often able to suggest the re-allocation of resources or the implementation of alternative timetables which reduced the subsidy requirement and thus nullified the benefits of the proposed transfer.

To the Tillingbourne Company, it seemed somewhat frustrating that all the proposals made over the previous ten years on the lines of route transfer had not materialised. Of the expansion achieved in Surrey by Tillingbourne, much of which had been with the active support of the County Council, virtually none had been through taking over unremunerative NBC routes. Nevertheless, following the protracted discussions concerning the future of the 425 route, it appeared to the Company that the County Council might be disposed towards giving serious consideration to a properly worked out scheme, provided that adequate time was allowed for discussion and consultation.

Less than a month after Surrey County Council indicated to Tillingbourne that further consideration of the future of route 425 would be postponed until 1984, Barry King wrote again on 2 June 1983. Referring to the Public Transport Plan Consultative Document issued by the County Council, in which there was a reference to possible reductions in Sunday services generally, and specifically to a withdrawal of the Sunday service operated by Alder Valley between Cranleigh and Horsham, Tillingbourne offered to operate the Sunday service between Guildford and Cranleigh (Park Mead) with no subsidy payment. The County Council responded by promising to put this idea to the Transportation Planning Joint Sub-Committee in July, and confirmed that a new approach might be necessary, and that various hypotheses were being studied which would be discussed with the Company later that year. Tillingbourne then produced a commercial timetable for Sunday services between Guildford and Horsham, which included diverting the Horsham service to operate via Rowhook to Ewhurst, and thus would no longer serve Rudgwick and Ellens Green. Barry King had also been carefully considering the implications of the correspondence from the County Council, and he now suggested that the time was right for serious consideration to be given to the idea of Tillingbourne taking over completely, on a self-supporting basis, the services between Guildford, Cranleigh and Horsham. This would include the operation of a circular route from Guildford via Wonersh, Cranleigh, Ewhurst, Gomshall and

**79. 898 FUF was the Guernsey Albion Victor acquired from a Preservationist in order to operate a Sunday Vintage bus service in 1983. The location is Shere Village. (G.Burnett)**

**80. Bedford YMT/Plaxton Bustler A889 FPM was similar to FOD 941Y, apart from the livery application, and was caught passing Horsham Arts Centre on service 451 in December 1984. (N.Gow)**

Chilworth combined with the withdrawal of the London Country service between Gomshall and Guildford via Chilworth, as previously discussed, and these services should be sufficiently profitable to cross-subsidise services to such places as Alfold and Walliswood. The point was also made that, with the intended sale of the Metropolitan subsidiary, sufficient finance would be available to fund such an expansion.

On 27 June, the County Council replied expressing interest in this proposal, but suggesting that the matter could not be viewed in isolation, but only in concert with other bus service activities in the Guildford area. Following upon this, Barry King arranged to meet the two other Guildford area independent bus operators, Safeguard Coaches and Blue Saloon, with a view to gauging their reaction to the idea of a joint approach to the County Council with a radical plan for the Guildford area which would offer the County Council attractive financial savings.

Further meetings followed at which the three independent operators decided on their proposals and agreed the necessary strategy. The plan which finally took shape allowed for all local bus services in the Guildford City area, together with all longer distance services using the Guildford, Cranleigh, Horsham corridor and the Guildford, Chilworth, Shere corridor to be transferred to the independent companies. While the Guildford City services would be divided between Safeguard and Blue Saloon, Tillingbourne would operate to the pattern described above, with some modifications which would allow for replacement services to such places as Alfold, Plaistow, Farley Green, Holmbury St.Mary and Forest Green. One of the proposals was for the introduction of a "Villager Minibus" service by Tillingbourne to replace certain rural routes. It was considered that this would be particularly attractive to local politicians, who had often called for the introduction of minibus services.

Whilst Alder Valley and London Country may have regarded such proposals as being so radical as not worthy of consideration by the County Council, the three independents were determined to demonstrate the rationale behind the plans. They claimed that, although the National Bus Company had been in existence for fifteen years at that time, little rationalisation between its two operating subsidiaries had take place in the Guildford area, despite the 1980 MAP exercise. They considered that many of the other services provided by Alder Valley could continue unaltered, whilst the residual activities of the Company in the Guildford area, were the independents' proposals to be implemented, could be handled by reallocation of a small number of vehicles to one or other of the two NBC garages in Guildford. The closure of a garage would thus bring about the necessary substantial reduction in fixed costs which would avoid any serious erosion of the anticipated revenue support savings.

It was difficult for the independent companies to calculate the savings which were likely to benefit the Local Authority, however information on the operating deficits of the various routes in the Guildford area was available. For the services mentioned above, the total operating defecit in the financial year 1982/83 was a staggering £501,000, and there was no reason to believe that the majority of this figure was not paid to the two NBC operators in the form of revenue support. It will thus be seen that, although the proposals were radical, the financial stakes were high. Of the three independent companies, only Tillingbourne received financial support from the County Council, and this amounted to an annual sum of £35,000, yet the network of routes which the companies operated were not dissimilar to those of the two NBC subsidiaries in terms of revenue yield. Bearing in mind the level of financial support, the independent companies considered that withdrawal of subsidy would automatically result in the transfer of the services in question, therefore they concentrated on the questions likely to be raised regarding their claimed lower operating costs, the ability to organise and fund the required expansion, the quality of the service which they could provide and the frequencies, routeings and timings of the proposed replacement services.

A further meeting with officers of Surrey County Council took place, and it was made clear that, were the County Council to agree to investigate the proposals and subsequently support them, the three independent operators were expected to stand by their plans, even if ultimately it resulted in a Traffic Court Hearing battle. Both Alder Valley and London Country were informed of the broad outlines of the proposals, and it was agreed that the plans would be presented to the County Council's Transportation Planning Joint Sub-Committee for consideration in November 1983.

Although the Consortium, as it came to be known, consisted of three equal partners, much of the co-ordination and presentation work had devolved upon Tillingbourne, and it was at this stage that the management team of Tillingbourne gave some considerable thought as to the best tactics to adopt in order to ensure the future progress of the proposals. Previously, such matters had been debated in confidence between the bus companies and officers of the County Council, however it was now decided to take the radical step of raising the debate to a political level and involving the local media. A meeting was requested and granted whereby the Consortium were allowed to make a presentation to a delegation of Members and Officers of the County Council in November 1983. In order to make this as professional as possible, a 50 page submission was produced, explaining the need for change, showing the proposals in detail including projected costings and savings, advancing reasons and evidence for the lower operating costs of the Consortium and detailing the impact which the proposals would have on the NBC companies and how it was intended to deal with such matters as the future operation of Guildford's Friary Bus Station.

On 11 January 1984, the Highways and Transport Committee of Surrey County Council agreed to make an in-depth study of future bus services in the Guildford/Cranleigh area by appointing outside consultants to prepare an impartial report on the issues involved. As anticipated, the NBC companies had presented alternative proposals based on taking over most of the Safeguard and Tillingbourne routes and operating them on some form of marginal costing which it was claimed would save the County Council subsidy. No indications were given as to how such a transfer could be effected for routes where no subsidy was paid, and the Members of the County Council, faced with proposals and counter-proposals, felt that the issues at stake were of such fundamental importance that expert and impartial advice was essential. In the meantime, the proposals had received much coverage in the local press. Both Alder Valley and London Country were alarmed by the plans and, recognising a distinct threat to the network subsidy principle so important to them, they set about analysing the independents' proposals and producing counter suggestions of their own. Although conscious of the challenge, both companies failed to grasp the reality of the lower operating costs claimed by the independents. Faced with an energetic and expanding company regularly purchasing new rolling stock, London Country's management, for example, claimed that Tillingbourne actually ran at a loss, and that future vehicle replacement could be a problem. The history of the Company since 1984 may be taken as evidence of the validity of this claim.

It had now become apparent that, with the consultants not being appointed until March and the Report unlikely to appear before August 1984, it would be a long time before any further decisions would be taken. Tillingbourne realised that the most important tasks facing the Company were to pursue the proposals in an efficient and professional manner with the chosen consultants, MVA Consultants Ltd.(in conjunction with PA Management Consultants Ltd.), and to ensure that staff morale remained high by means of keeping them as fully informed as possible concerning what must have been very unsettling events for the staff of all the bus operators involved in the proposed changes.

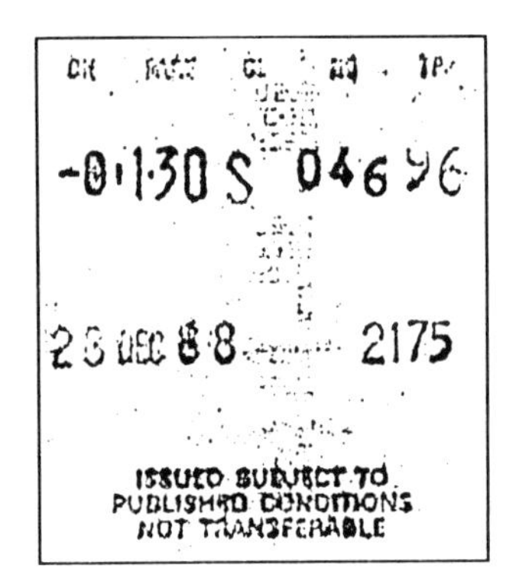


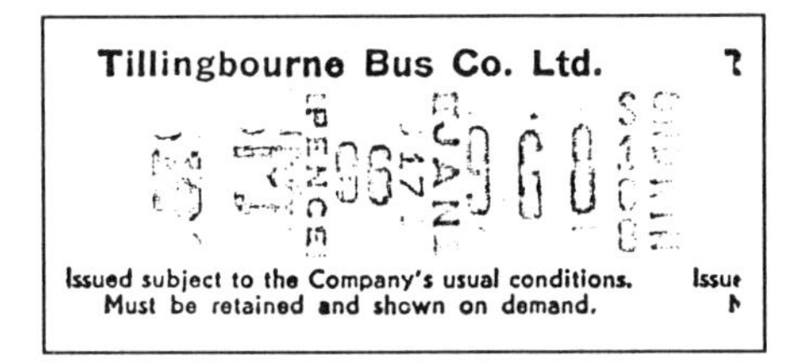


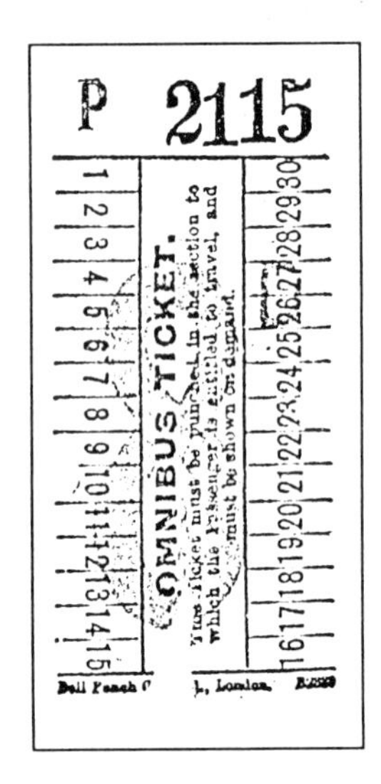

# CHAPTER 8 - PLANNING FOR THE FUTURE

It will be recalled that, at the time when Trevor Brown purchased the Company from the Trice family, a number of driving staff had been with the Tillingbourne Company for some years, amongst whom were Jim Hatcher, Bert Woolgar and Jack Taverner. They continued in employment through the ups and downs of the early 1970s, however one by one they retired so that by the early 1980s, only Peter Birch, who had been employed by Derek Trice as an apprentice in 1964, remained of the original Trice employees. Nevertheless, the Company enjoyed a good management/staff relationship in the 1980s, with several of the drivers, such as Jack Ahern, Brian Kingsford and Rodney Trout, having been with Tillingbourne for a number of years. Some came from the local NBC companies, finding the hours and the conditions of employment more congenial, whilst others were former coach drivers who had decided that the more regular hours associated with bus driving were preferable to the variety and uncertainty of coach driving. Barry King had, firstly, become the General Manager of Tillingbourne, and then, after being appointed a director, assumed the role of Managing Director, with Trevor Brown adopting the title of Chairman of the Tillingbourne Group of Companies. By 1983, Chris Bowler had become the Company's Chief Engineer, and his brother, Kenny, was also employed as a mechanic/coach driver.

In September 1983, more complaints were made to Tillingbourne's staff by passengers who had experienced difficulties when trying to use their Tillingbourne return tickets on London Country and Alder Valley buses. Having failed to resolve this problem through conventional channels, this time Barry King took the radical step of deciding no longer to accept other operators' return tickets. Although it undoubtedly inconvenienced the public to a degree, it was a shrewd move as it obliged passengers to think carefully which bus company's service they would use in order to have the most convenient return journey, and with Tillingbourne now the dominant operator on the Gomshall to Guildford section of road, there is evidence that it resulted in an increase in passenger loadings for Tillingbourne.

Before Christmas in 1982, Alan Brown, one of Tillingbourne's former Southdown drivers, had driven several of his shifts dressed in a borrowed Father Christmas outfit, handing out sweets to children, and this had been very popular with passengers. For 1983 the Company gave official sanction to this and purchased an outfit for Alan to wear, and, ever since, Father Christmas driving a Tillingbourne bus has been an annual event. In 1983, a special leaflet was produced in conjunction with the Hurtwood Inn at Peaslake offering discounted travel for those purchasing the special Christmas meal available at this Trust House Forte hotel, together with the offer of free presentation packs of German white wine, which would be distributed at random to Tillingbourne passengers by the Managing Director and the Traffic Manager. The cover design incorporated a cartoon depicting a Tillingbourne bus flying through the snow towed by reindeer, whilst a dejected figure was shown endeavouring to dig his unmistakably Alder Valley bus out of a snowdrift! Whilst all this had the desired effect of boosting staff morale, at the time, a dim view of it was taken by both Alder Valley staff and management, who did not appreciate the joke.

In the Horsham area, builders were completing a new housing estate called Hills Farm which was just off the road from Broadbridge Heath to Horsham Town Centre. In January 1984, Tillingbourne applied for a road service licence variation to serve Hills Farm by means of diverting most journeys between these points and thus rearranging the general timetable for service 450. This application was approved, and in March the driving staff were told by means of a memo that the service would start in April/May, and that the Company had managed to beat the NBC operators in serving this estate. However, the diversion never actually took place because of a reassessment of the number of potential passengers and because, with the Guildford/Cranleigh Study at a crucial stage, it was considered an inappropriate time to make such changes.

**81. The Leyland Tiger/Duple Dominant bus B877 OLJ was purchased from a Dealer's new stock and is an exceptionally lively performer. It was posed for the camera on Cranleigh Common. (G.Burnett)**

With all efforts being concentrated on the outcome of the Study, the whole of 1984 saw remarkably few changes in the Company's services. The Tuesday journey of route 454 to Brighton and Worthing had always been a seasonal route, with high summer loadings cross subsidising the lower winter usage. Loadings had been declining, however, partly because the service no longer had any novelty value and partly because Alder Valley had commenced operating a summer only service between Cranleigh and Brighton which, because of its direct routeing, abstracted a number of passengers from the Tillingbourne service. Consequently, West Sussex

County Council was approached for financial assistance, and when this was not forthcoming, the service was withdrawn in July 1984. At the same time the afternoon schooldays journey of route 454 was terminated at Alfold Crossways instead of Cranleigh, and the Thursday shopping journey of route 450 from Ockley to Forest Green, and thence to Guildford via route 446, was also withdrawn due to limited patronage.

The year 1984 marked Tillingbourne's 60th anniversary. At the time of the 50th anniversary in 1974, Barry King had researched and produced a short history of the Company and there was some debate as to how best to commemorate this latest anniversary. Early in the year, the Company was approached by Model Road and Rail of Worcester Park, a shop specialising in retailing special edition model buses. One of the proprietors lived in Peaslake, and they were seeking permission to commission a special edition version of a typical small single decker bus of the late 1920s or early 1930s in Tillingbourne livery. This seemed to the Company an excellent way of celebrating the Diamond Jubilee, and not only was permission granted but assistance was provided in ensuring the use of the authentic maroon livery and scroll type fleetname and 600 of the production run were ordered by Tillingbourne, which were sold complete with commemorative gold stickers with the limited edition number and an insert in the box with notes on the Company's history and comparative route maps. This proved so popular that a further supply of these Lledo models in Tillingbourne livery were purchased for retail, many being offered for sale on the Company's service buses, with the drivers earning commission on their sale.

In July 1984, the Government published a White Paper entitled "Buses", which was eventually to change radically the whole process of bus service provision through means of deregulation and privatisation. The Consultants were four-fifths through their work in the Guildford/Cranleigh Study when the White Paper appeared, and there was some debate as to what effect the Government's proposals would have on the Study findings. Tillingbourne was concerned that the County Council might take no action on the findings of the Study and await government legislation. However, the Consultants' Report was published in September and the findings generally confirmed the views of the independent operators that there could be significant financial savings, that the companies were aware of the changes they would need to make, and the "inescapable" costs for the NBC companies would not be as significant as had been claimed by Alder Valley and London Country.

The recommendations which emerged from the Report were that the County Council should seek to implement the Safeguard and Tillingbourne proposals, enhanced by fine tuning in certain respects, as rapidly as practicable through negotiation with the NBC companies. This should be accompanied by the phasing out of Tillingbourne's revenue support and Blue Saloon's proposals should only be implemented on the receipt of certain assurances concerning improved management accounting practices and guarantees regarding the availability of capital necessary to finance expansion. It was recommended that the County Council should try to avoid changes to school contracts affecting the independent companies in the short term, and that the companies should give guarantees that the Consortium would operate as promised, particularly regarding the areas of public relations, marketing and publicity.

On the face of things, Tillingbourne's proposals seemed to have been entirely vindicated, however, in reality, the problems for the companies were only just beginning, as implementation proved to be a more difficult task than had persuading the County Council to look in depth at the proposals in the first place. In addition, several parts of the Report were not entirely to the advantage of the Tillingbourne concern. The phasing out of revenue support would only be acceptable if the Company was successful in implementing profitable services at the expense of Alder Valley. The Consultants had recommended the retention of London Country's 425 service, with the proposed Tillingbourne circular service being rerouted via Newlands Corner and Merrow. This latter conclusion was particularly difficult for the Company to understand, as the financial problems of the 425 could have been said to have been responsible for setting the whole scheme into motion. The reduction in frequency of the Albury and Chilworth route to an hourly Tillingbourne service had been a central feature in ensuring financial viability for services in the Tillingbourne Valley, and the Company considered that Guildford to Dorking traffic could be catered for by the 762 semi-express service.

The Consultants' Report was presented to the County Council's Transportation Planning Joint Sub-Committee and approved in October 1984, with the recommendation that the County Council should request the three independent operators and the two NBC companies to enter into negotiations intended to implement the Study Proposals with the understanding that no subsidy would be forthcoming for any of the bus services in the areas under consideration, this latter stipulation being intended to put pressure on the parties to reach an accommodation as soon as possible. Whilst it seemed most unlikely that the NBC companies would simply continue to operate their services without the subsidy of almost half a million pounds received annually, it also served to demonstrate that, despite the co-ordination role of the County Council, the one thing that the Authority was unable to do was order the transfer of routes from one company to another.

Throughout October and November 1984, a series of bi-partite talks took place between the various operators. Interestingly, discussions involving London Country proceded very smoothly. It was apparent that the chief concern of that company was the operation of the Merrow area routes and the maintenance of some form of direct Guildford to Dorking service. When it became apparent that Blue Saloon would be likely to benefit from a transfer of some of Alder Valley's services, the former company indicated that it would be prepared not to pursue the idea of taking over the Merrow area routes. At the same time, Alder Valley had shown some disinterest in continuing its share of the 762 service, and thus London Country saw the possibility of recasting the service as an approximately hourly joint operation with Southdown between Brighton and Guildford only. An agreement in principle was reached between Tillingbourne and London Country whereby the 425 would be withdrawn, Tillingbourne would operate a "Villager Minibus" service on Mondays to Fridays to replace the 412 route in the off-peak and extend it to Shere to connect with the main Guildford service, with London Country continuing to operate the two peak buses required on the 412 for school movements. On Saturdays it was agreed that service provision would be by three return Tillingbourne through journeys between Guildford and Dorking via Chilworth,

Shere and Holmbury St.Mary. The "Villager Minibus" would provide a Fridays only facility for Ranmore to replace the 425, and the Summers only 417 "Ramblers Bus" would continue to be operated by London Country.

Of all the companies involved in discussions, undoubtedly the most difficult decisions had to be made by Alder Valley. If Alder Valley wished to continue to have a major presence in the Guildford/Cranleigh areas, fairly radical changes in order to lower operating costs would be essential, whilst at the same time some form of agreement with the independent operators was also preferable in order to avoid the attrition of a competitive situation. Alder Valley had already made an extensive analysis of its own operations and confirmed that the Cranleigh to Guildford corridor was its most potentially profitable area of operation. At this stage, Alder Valley commissioned their own consultants, Colin Buchanan & Partners, to prepare a report with recommendations in the light of the Study Report. Buchanans appear to have confirmed Alder Valley's views that a strong presence in the Guildford - Cranleigh corridor was essential, as were measures to cut operating costs. The consultants also thought it was unlikely that Tillingbourne would carry out its threat to compete in this corridor if Alder Valley were to stand firm. Thus the company adopted a strategy of trying to reach some form of agreement on the Guildford town services which would eliminate potential conflict with Blue Saloon and Safeguard, while simplifying and strengthening the main service between Guildford and Cranleigh via Shalford, Bramley, Wonersh and Shamley Green and endeavouring to prevent any incursion by Tillingbourne in this area. At the same time, plans which

**82. A coach suitable for all Tillingbourne's various activities was B124 PEL, a Bedford YNT with Plaxton Paramount body, also seen at Cranleigh Common. Shortly afterwards, the livery was further improved by the application of blue "lining out" on the yellow. (G.Burnett)**

were claimed to be already in existence to reduce operating costs were activated, although it seems certain that these were accelerated by the circumstances of the situation.

Negotiations between Tillingbourne and Alder Valley were far from successful, with Alder Valley making it quite clear that they intended to maintain a comprehensive service between Guildford and Cranleigh. By December 1984 the two sides had reached a stalemate, despite several suggestions at compromise solutions from Tillingbourne. The minimum aspirations of Tillingbourne consisted of an hourly circular service, preferably via Shamley Green, Wonersh and Bramley, whilst all that Alder Valley were prepared to concede was a less than hourly frequency service via Nanhurst Corner and Grafham. At this stage it became clear how Alder Valley intended to reduce operating costs in the area. The major independent coach operator in the Cranleigh district, Gastonia, had decided to cut down operations to just two or three vehicles and Alder Valley took this opportunity of not only acquiring the two commuter services to London operated by Gastonia, but also, and more significantly, to lease the premises occupied by them in Cranleigh and, thus, eventually be in a position to close the main garage in Woodbridge Road, Guildford, leaving just a small number of buses based at the Friary Bus Station. Paradoxically, this represented the type of cost saving operational measure advocated by the Consortium in their original proposals. In late December Alder Valley wrote to the County Council confirming their intention of leasing the premises at Manfield Park, Cranleigh, which would enable them to operate broadly the then current level of services in the area without revenue support. The County Council was also warned that the introduction of any form of competition in that area would probably lead to the withdrawal of the more unremunerative services. At the same time, Tillingbourne wrote to Alder Valley stating that it was apparent to the Company that Alder Valley had no intention of reaching a compromise agreement for the joint operation of services between Cranleigh and Guildford. It appeared that full scale competition could break out leading to instability and the possible withdrawal of services to areas such as Grafham, Alfold and Plaistow. It should be remembered that, at this time the County Council had a co-ordinating role to play, and that in the event of competitive applications, the County would need to decide which company's proposals it intended to support. Although it could be argued that Alder Valley was the established operator in the area, the County Council was obviously concerned over past payments made forrevenue support and obligations which the Authority had to support the implementation of the findings of the Consultants' Study.

Not surprisingly, both Alder Valley and Tillingbourne made applications to the Traffic Commissioners for completely revised service networks in February 1985, and both companies registered objections to the other's proposals. Along the hotly disputed corridor between Cranleigh and Guildford via Shamley Green, Wonersh and Bramley, Alder Valley proposed to operate a twenty minute frequency service and Tillingbourne a half-hourly service. The County Council asked Tillingbourne whether the Company would be prepared to implement its agreement with London Country, but not operate the services competing with Alder Valley. When the answer was received that this was not logistically possible by this stage, the County indicated that it would support the Tillingbourne applications at the Traffic Court

Hearing. Nevertheless the situation was of considerable concern to the Local Authority, as a Court Hearing would push the implementation way beyond the chosen date of 14 April 1985, which would have had serious implications for the continued payment of revenue support into the new financial year. Consequently there was a great deal of renewed pressure for the two bus companies to reach some form of mutually acceptable formula, even if a full agreement was impossible.

**83. To assist with additional work after the April 1985 service revisions, a pair of AEC Reliance buses were acquired from Hutchison of Overtown in Scotland. A day behind the wheel of one of these buses was quite hard work, and Author George Burnett is seen here with UGB 12R on route 25 at Guildford. (A.A.Thomas)**

From this situation, an agreement to accept each other's registrations but to operate on a competitive basis was reached during March 1985. Tillingbourne agreed to reduce the proposed frequency along the main corridor from half-hourly to hourly, to refrain from competing for the "school pass" traffic along that corridor, not to pursue the request for a stand within the main part of the Friary Bus Station and to reduce the frequency of the proposed Sunday service between Cranleigh and Guildford and, at the same time, to reroute the service via Grafham. Journeys between Guildford and Birtley Road, Bramley were to be shared fairly evenly between the companies, with Alder Valley retaining just peak hour journeys via Nanhurst Corner. Unlike the Guildford local services, there was no agreement to accept the other company's return tickets.

Neither company proposed services for Smithwood Common or New Road, Wonersh, however the County Council requested both companies to quote for a suitable provision. Such diversions would not have been attractive for Alder Valley, who set great store in their regular twenty minute headway service along the main corridor, consequently Tillingbourne secured agreement with the County Council whereby alternate journeys of the hourly circular service would operate via either Smithwood Common or New Road, Wonersh. In the light of the inability of Tillingbourne to cross subsidise services because of the competitive situation, the County Council agreed to pay a subsidy for the operation of the evening and Sunday services between Guildford and Gomshall via Shalford, Chilworth, Albury and Shere, together with the "Villager" minibus service.

Thus the new set of Tillingbourne services due to commence on 14 April 1985 represented the most radical single change in the Company's history. Apart from certain peak hour journeys, there was to be no regular Tillingbourne service over Newlands Corner and Merrow into Guildford, however the Company would be the sole operator through Albury and Chilworth with the new hourly circular service. One early morning journey of London Country route 412 would commence from Shere, however, apart from this, Tillingbourne would operate the only bus services in Shere as the new hourly 773 route, marketed as the "Sealine" service, did not operate via Shere Village, continuing to use the by-pass, as had its predecessor, route 762. Tillingbourne would also become the only operator in the off-peak period in the Sutton Abinger, Holmbury St.Mary and Abinger Common areas with the new "Villager Minibus" service. Limited facilities would remain for Forest Green and Farley Green, whilst, of course, the Company would appear for the first time on a regular basis in such places as Bramley, Wonersh, Shamley Green and Grafham. To market this expanded network, Tillingbourne took the radical step of completely renumbering the services. The use of London Country type numbers in the "400" series was becoming increasingly irrelevant, particularly as London Country themselves were using similar numbers close to Tillingbourne's operating territory, an example being the use of 451 in the Dorking area. It was considered that resurrecting the old numbers used by East Surrey and Aldershot & District would give the Company a distinctive identity, whilst at the same time pre-empting the opposition by utilising a numbering identity which they might have considered to be their heritage.

Thus the "Tillingbourne Villager" service was numbered 22, operating between Dorking Station and Shere, via Dorking, Westcott, Abinger Common, Holmbury St.Mary, Sutton, Abinger Hammer and Gomshall, with certain journeys operating via Forest Green. Approximately five journeys per day were made in each direction, the majority of which connected at Shere with the main service to Guildford. As mentioned previously, on Saturdays service 22 operated three return journeys from Guildford to Dorking via Chilworth. The circular hourly service was numbered 23 when operating between Ewhurst and Guildford via Cranleigh, Shamley Green, Wonersh and Bramley, and 25 when operating from Cranleigh to Guildford via Ewhurst, Peaslake, Gomshall, Shere, Albury, and Chilworth. Consequently, the route number was changed at Ewhurst when operating in a clockwise direction, and at Cranleigh when operating in an anti-clockwise direction. The limited number of journeys operating to Farley Green were also numbered 25. A limited evening service was operated on both services 23 and 25, which gave a late evening departure from Guildford to Peaslake for the first time for many years, and there was a two hourly Sunday service of route 25 between Gomshall and Guildford. Peak journeys were worked to Farley Green by diversion of the normal 25 service, whilst in the off peak there was a lunchtime journey provided by the minibus operating the "Villager" service with a connection at Albury. On Fridays, a special journey of service 25

**84. To operate the new "Villager" service 22 to Dorking, a 16 seat Ford Transit with Dixon Lomas body conversion was purchased in April 1985. B49 TVR was posed at Holmbury St. Mary soon after arrival and before the service had started operation. (G.Burnett)**

operated from Ockley to Guildford, via Oakwoodhill, Walliswood, Ewhurst Green, Ewhurst, Peaslake (although never advertised to serve that village), Shere Heath, Little London, Farley Green, Albury, Blackheath, Chilworth and Shalford. Service 33 operated from Guildford to Cranleigh approximately 4/5 times daily, via Shalford, Bramley, Grafham, Nanhurst Corner and West Cranleigh, with peak hour extensions to Park Mead via Glebe Road. On Sundays, three return journeys of service 33 operated from Ewhurst to Guildford, reinstating a Sunday service for Ewhurst. The peak hour journeys from Cranleigh to Guildford operated via Newlands Corner and Merrow were numbered 44. Service 444, which ran on schooldays only between Cranleigh and Dorking, was withdrawn, although the school contract journeys operated by minibus between Friday Street, Broadmoor and Dorking were worked as part of service 22. The Horsham area services simply had the "4" removed from their number, thus becoming 50, 51, 52 and 54. Journeys of service 50 via Warnham Station were renumbered as 53, the Saturday service of route 50 being reduced with no through workings from Guildford and the Fridays shopping service via Ockley and Rowhook was withdrawn. Service 54 journeys from

Horsham were extended to Cranleigh, however in most other respects, there were few changes to services in the Horsham area.

Planning the fleet and staffing requirements for the new services had been a difficult task with the uncertainty surrounding the implementation of the proposals. Nevertheless, during 1984 the Company had purchased no fewer than four new full sized vehicles. Two further Bedford YMT buses with Plaxton Bustler bodywork, A 889 FPM and B 327 KPD were added to the fleet, similar to FOD 941 Y apart from having a standard application of the paint scheme. Although these new Bedfords were nearer to the ideal than previous lightweight vehicles, the Company was still interested in standardising on a new heavyweight chassis. Initial reliability problems with the Dennis Dorchester buses, together with the restriction of having to use Wadham Stringer bodywork (which did not wear so well as Plaxton or Duple bus bodywork) led Tillingbourne to look at other alternatives. A Leyland Tiger 245 with Duple Dominant bus body, B 877 OLJ, was purchased from Yeates, the bus and coach dealers, from stock. This powerful bus, capable of ascending Newlands Corner in fifth gear, was certainly a far cry from the Tiger Cubs and Bristol SULs that were the standard vehicles of the early 1970s. Tillingbourne was also looking at purchasing a flagship coach, as private hire work had been increasing steadily, and was to continue to do so after the demise of most of the Gastonia fleet. Consequently, another stock vehicle was purchased from Yeates in the shape of B 124 PEL, a Bedford YNT with Plaxton Paramount bodywork. Delivered in the usual coach livery of yellow ochre and Danube blue, the appearance of this coach was soon further improved by the application of blue lining out. The two Bedfords acquired from Gipsey Queen were sold during 1984, as were the last of the 10 metre length Bedfords, WPL 985 S and EPH 27 V, together with the hybrid Leyland Tiger coach, TPL 762 X.

By the end of 1984, the fleet strength was reduced slightly to 17 vehicles, three of which were leased to Metrobus and one, the Albion Victor, which was in storage, with the average age being a healthy two years. Once the plans for the new services commencing in April 1985 became firm, the Company employed an additional fitter, one of several staff from Southdown's Horsham depot who left at this time, and two additional drivers. The pit at Littlemead was extended to double length to enable two vehicles to be worked on simultaneously, and the main garage was reroofed. On the vehicle front, two buses were required urgently, together with a more suitable minibus than the Ford Transit with standard bodywork then operated. Tillingbourne chose a Ford Transit 16 seater bus, B 49 TVR, supplied by Dixon Lomas (Made to Measure), which arrived in a yellow and blue livery with the fleetname "Tillingbourne Villager". Two second hand AEC Reliance buses with Duple Dominant bodywork and manual gearboxes were purchased as a stop-gap measure from Hutchinsons of Overtown, UGB 12 & 14 R. Although Surrey County Council produced an excellent Guildford area timetable to publicise the new network, Tillingbourne decided to market its own services by producing a striking timetable which featured the new Leyland Tiger bus on the front cover and included a network map on the back page.

# CHAPTER 9 - CO-ORDINATED COMPETITION

The new services duly commenced on 14 April 1985 with relatively few teething problems considering the extent of the changes. The initial day of operation caused considerable local interest, with the management of the bus companies much in evidence, together with staff from the County Council. While the public were becoming familiar with the new routes and, in some cases unfamiliar operators, the bus companies began the task of monitoring the performance and reliability of both their own and the other companies, Alder Valley even going to the length of having an observer stationed at Millbrook in Guildford for the first couple of weeks checking the loadings of all buses entering and leaving the town. From Tillingbourne's point of view, it soon became apparent that revenue was considerably enhanced, particularly in the Tillingbourne Valley, however work would be needed to capture a significant percentage of traffic on the main corridor from Cranleigh to Guildford. Nevertheless, the new network was judged to be a considerable success for the Company, placing it in a good position to tackle the challenges soon to be faced with Deregulation.

Despite careful study of the loading figures for the erstwhile 412 service, some difficulties were experienced with the replacement "Villager" minibus service, route 22. There was some disquiet from residents of Chilworth and Albury that their links with Dorking had almost disappeared, and some of the timings of the 22 service were criticised by users from Holmbury St.Mary and Abinger Common. Nevertheless, the greatest problem turned out to be one of capacity. On the second day of operation, the novelty aspect of the minibus service led to a standing load on some of the more popular shopping journeys, together with difficulties created by a minority of London Country staff at Dorking Garage, who resented the Tillingbourne service using the Bus Station located on the forecourt of the garage, despite official sanction having been received from Head Office in Reigate. Whilst the latter problem was soon dealt with by managerial action from both companies, the former was to reappear at odd times over the next few months. Tuesdays and Fridays were soon recognised as days when larger numbers of passengers were likely to materialise, whilst the 1735 hrs departure from Dorking was sometimes very popular. During the summer months, parties of Brownies from Holmbury, unaware that the bus service had been converted to minibus operation, and those arriving at Dorking station in numbers to travel to conference/study facilities offered by a school near Abinger Common also added to difficulties. Of course, these problems could be exaggerated; Surrey County Council received a vociferous complaint concerning the reliability and overcrowding on the Tillingbourne service within a few days of 14 April allegedly from the husband of a lady from Holmbury St.Mary who used the service regularly. However, on investigation by Tillingbourne management, the address given turned out to be occupied by a elderly housebound widow, who had not used the bus services for many months, but who suggested that any problems to do with buses could be resolved by speaking to her son, who was a London Country driver at Dorking!

The Company dealt with these problems by operating a 10 metre vehicle on days when it was anticipated that there would be extra usage, however from 27 October

1985 larger vehicles were used on all route 22 journeys, except for the special school journeys which operated via Friday Street and Broadmoor. Thus Tillingbourne's first flirtation with true minibus operation was not a success, although it could be argued that the 16 seater van conversion was not the right size and type of vehicle for the service. This bus also suffered from some design problems, the most serious being the lack of ventilation in hot weather. Significantly, the next purchase of minibuses in 1986 specified sliding windows, so some lessons were learnt from the experiment.

The other problem facing the Company was that of encouraging customers to use the new services operating between Cranleigh and Guildford via Bramley. Whilst residents of Smithwood Common and the New Road area of Wonersh simply switched to the Tillingbourne services from necessity, the Company had a degree of success in capturing traffic from Alder Valley from such areas as Nanhurst Corner, Grafham and the southern area of Bramley, persuading residents of such areas as Rowly, Shamley Green and Wonersh to switch their allegiance from Alder Valley when Tillingbourne only operated an hourly service against the competition's three buses per hour proved to be slow. Whilst the loadings achieved compared reasonably well with some other parts of the Company's area of operations, it was recognised that there was some potential to increase the attractiveness of the Tillingbourne services without increasing frequencies. Consequently, a concerted effort was made to increase patronage from October 1985, firstly by attacking the market from the Ewhurst area where Tillingbourne's level of service provision compared favourably with that of Alder Valley, and, secondly, by competitive pricing where the Company's services were less attractive to potential users. This latter tactic was, to some degree, a response to Alder Valley's introduction of "saver strips", which were pre-purchased tickets offering a free journey, thus encouraging passengers to use their services for the duration of the "strip". Tillingbourne produced a leaflet entitled, "Big Bargains on the Blue Buses" which stressed the competitive nature of the Company's ordinary fares, offered two new discount schemes, the "Cost-Cutter" four-weekly ticket giving unlimited travel on services 23 and 33 plus free travel for one accompanied child at weekends, and the "Shopper-Saver", available after 0845 hrs which, in the case of Ewhurst, was 30p cheaper than the normal return fare. The leaflet also had a tear off corner offering 10p off the next bus journey, and a house to house distribution was arranged around the Ewhurst area.

A new timetable was published at the same time, which incorporated some minor changes, including an extra evening journey from Guildford on service 25 at 1920 hrs and other minor improvements. Interestingly, for the first time in several years, this timetable reverted to use of the 24 hour clock. Tillingbourne was among those companies who felt that the public was more at ease with am and pm times, however, as the crew duties etc were all given in 24 hour format, it became increasingly irksome to have to "convert" so many timetables from one format to the other, so the opportunity was taken to publish all information in 24 hour format.

The response to the actions mentioned above was encouraging, except in the case of Ewhurst, which might have reflected the total number of those travelling from the village rather than the persuasive powers of the Company's literature! One difficulty which remained unresolved was the inability of the Company, in some

**85. JDE 189 X was a Leyland Tiger/Duple coach which came from Silcox of Pembroke Dock in July 1985. It is recorded here at Friary Bus Station working route 33. (P.R.Nuttall)**

**86. Between Shalford and Guildford there is competition for traffic. Behind Tillingbourne's Leyland Tiger C195 WJT is an Alder Valley Leyland National. To confuse the drivers, this bus has a right handed selection for the semi-automatic gearchange, whilst its similar but more powerful sister vehicle, B 877 OLJ, has a left handed change. (L.James)**

areas, to provide roadside publicity. London Country had agreed to sell all the bus stops which their routes no longer served, thus the majority in the Tillingbourne Valley area passed to the Company, however Alder Valley not only refused permission for Tillingbourne to display information at their bus stops, but also attached their own timetable frames to virtually every stop in the Guildford/Cranleigh area. Unfortunately for Tillingbourne, the stops between Shalford and Guildford, which had been owned by London Country, were passed to Alder Valley under the terms of an internal NBC agreement governing such matters. Tillingbourne used every available piece of neighbouring street furniture to attach timetable frames, but undoubtedly laboured under a significant disadvantage in this matter.

On the vehicle front, the two AEC Reliance buses purchased as a stop gap measure were both sold by the end of 1985, one, UGB 14 R, going to Safeguard, who had not operated any AEC vehicles for some years. Another connection with Safeguard was the purchase of a new Leyland Tiger with Duple Dominant bus bodywork, C 195 WJT; the order for this and a virtually identical bus for Safeguard having been made together in order to improve vehicle delivery times. The other vehicle purchased during 1985 was a secondhand Leyland Tiger coach with Duple Dominant coachwork, JDE 189 X, from the fleet of Silcox of Pembroke Dock, thus confirming the popularity of the Leyland Tiger with Tillingbourne at this time.

Under the arrangements made by central government for the implementation of the Transport Act, all companies wishing to operate local bus services (a simple term replacing the archaic "stage carriage service") from 26 October 1986 onwards were required to register such services during the month of February 1986. These would not, of course, be subject to any subsidy from local authorities. It was then the task of local authorities to examine all such registrations and to decide, after a consultation period, whether to put out to competitive tender any additional local bus services deemed to be of a socially necessary nature. One small exception to the competitive tendering process was the ability of local authorities to enter into direct agreements with operators to secure services, provided that each single agreement did not exceed £4,000 per annum and that total agreements between one local authority and one operator did not exceed £20,000 per annum.

Both operators and local authorities waited with bated breath to see who had registered what services. As far as Tillingbourne was concerned, there were, initially, few real surprises. The clockwise circular services 23 and 25 were reduced to a basic two-hourly frequency, with most 23 journeys serving Wonersh, New Road. Anti-clockwise journeys of the circular service were usually formed by service 33 journeys, which latter route was thus extended to Ewhurst, continuing to Guildford as route 25. On 24 March 1986, certain journeys of route 33 were diverted to operate via the Retirement Homes Association's premises at Nanhurst, as had certain Alder Valley journeys, and this diversion was reflected in the registration for service 33. As Alder Valley did not register any services via Grafham and Nanhurst Corner, the Tillingbourne presence on this corridor was strengthened, while, at the same time, the Company's presence on the main routeing via Shamley Green and Wonersh was lessened. In order to retain the hourly frequency between Guildford and Gomshall via Shalford, Chilworth, Albury and Shere, service 22 was registered on a basic two-hourly frequency between Guildford and Dorking, with most journeys operating via Holmbury St.Mary and Abinger Common. The one or two odd journeys which still operated via Newlands Corner were numbered as route 22 or 25, thus the 44 route number disappeared. London Country and Brighton & Hove had registered the 773 service, similar in routeing but with slightly fewer journeys. Alder Valley had registered their services between Guildford and Cranleigh in an almost identical form, although, as mentioned above, there were no journeys via Grafham and neither were any services registered on the 269 route to Loxwood and Plaistow or the 246 route between Godalming and Cranleigh via Busbridge, Hascombe and Dunsfold.

In this area there was a small surprise in that Tillingbourne registered two services, routes 43 and 46, between Cranleigh and Godalming. Route 43 operated via Knowle Lane, Alfold Crossways, Alfold, Loxwood, Plaistow, Durfold Wood, Dunsfold, Hascombe and Busbridge two or three times per day, Mondays to Fridays, while route 46 operated via Nanhurst Corner, Dunsfold, and then the 43 routeing three times a day on Mondays to Fridays. The 46 had a peak hour facility into Godalming, however the 43 only had a pm peak hour return from Guildford and Cranleigh. On Saturdays, a truncated version of the service was registered with no journeys between Dunsfold and Godalming. Most journeys either extended into Guildford via the 23 or 33 routes, or direct connections with through fares were arranged. Hardly surprisingly, the Company did not register any services on evenings or Sundays.

In the Horsham area, the 51 service was registered in its entirety together with journeys from and to Cranleigh in the morning and early evening peaks of services 50 and 53, although the routeing of the latter two services was unusual in being via Ockley and Forest Green instead of Oakwoodhill and Walliswood. The Tuesday and Saturday shopping services of route 50 were also registered, although the former was to start at Ewhurst instead of Forest Green, and was not to operate via Rowhook. It was already the intention to cease operation of the peak hour journeys of service 54 in July 1986, at the end of the school term, thus neither these nor the Friday only shopping service were registered, nor was the 52 service between Lambs Green, Rusper and Horsham.

Once all the commercial registrations were examined, a few surprises were evident. London Country (soon to become London Country Bus (South West) Ltd. with the split up of the company into four components) had registered very little in the Dorking area other than the 773 mentioned above and the 714 Greenline route from Horsham to Victoria. When this became apparent to Tillingbourne, the Company saw an opportunity to expand its commercial operation by extending the 22 route from Dorking Station to Newdigate via Brockham, Strood Green and Leigh. The registered timetable was permitted to be altered to incorporate 4/5 return journeys per day to Newdigate (with the first and last journeys operating from/to Cranleigh in service) and a regular hourly off-peak service as far as Strood Green. It would appear that this move did not endear the Company to London Country, who still thought in "territorial" terms and no doubt were hoping to pick up this service along with other routes in the Dorking area. Consequently, when Surrey County Council issued tenders for the evening and Sunday service between Guildford and Dorking via the Valley road and for a Mondays to Fridays peak service between Farley Green and Guildford with a Tuesdays and Fridays off-peak shopping facility, they were all awarded to London Country, who had submitted particularly favourable quotations.

By July and August 1986 when the tenders were being issued, Surrey County Council had decided to number contract services for the most part in the series 500-599, in order to identify supported services to the general public. Thus the Guildford to Dorking service was numbered 525 and the Farley Green service 545. This arrangement did not apply to services secured by use of the "De Minimis" provisions of the Transport Act, of which several were negotiated with Tillingbourne. Thus the peak hour 50 and 53 journeys were re-routed to operate via Walliswood and Oakwoodhill, the off-peak 50 journey was to start at Forest Green, an additional early evening peak journey was to operate from Dorking to Guildford, service 23 journeys were diverted to operate via Smithwood Common, enhancements to the services between Cranleigh and Godalming were provided as services 43 and 46 and a peak hour journey of service 25 was to be provided from Cranleigh to Guildford via Merrow for George Abbot School.

In addition to the services mentioned above, London Country South West secured several contracts for the Dorking area, which included service 549 between Chart Downs and Goodwyns Estate via Dorking with additional peak hour and evening journeys to and from Westcott and Strood Green, an extension of the 414 service from Reigate to Dorking, Goodwyns Estate on all days of the week, a single morning peak journey between Dorking and Guildford via Westcott, Abinger Hammer, Gomshall, Newlands Corner and Merrow numbered 573 and an early moring 525 journey from Shere to Dorking via Holmbury St.Mary and Abinger Common. The two peak hour schools buses operated on service 412 by London Country were replaced by one commercial journey of Tillingbourne 22 and a 512 service from Ockley to Dorking, initially awarded to Tillingbourne but in the event operated on hire to Tillingbourne by Austins Coaches of Dorking. London Country were certainly not completely successful in the Dorking area as there were two further operators new to the area, Epsom Coaches who won the 551 service between Dorking and Boxhill (with odd 570 journeys between Dorking and Leatherhead) and Southdown, whose Horsham Depot operated a peak hours school journey of service 570 between Capel and Epsom.

In two other areas of Surrey Tillingbourne expanded their operational area through winning contracts. The Sunday version of Alder Valley's commercial 271 service between Chiddingfold and Guildford via Witley, Milford and Godalming was awarded to the Company as route 571. Of more interest, two local services operating between Reigate and Redhill, the former 447 route operating via Meadvale and Earlswood and the 487 route via Batts Hill were also awarded to Tillingbourne as services 547 and 587. The original intention of the County Council was to have one vehicle operating a ninety minute frequency, however Tillingbourne offered to operate an hourly off-peak service as an attractive option at no additional cost by utilising a bus between its school contract requirements. In addition, the contract included a morning peak journey between Whitebushes Estate and Redhill to fill a gap in the timetable of London Country's route 411. The Saturday service between Cranleigh and Dunsfold was enhanced by further contract journeys which included a limited facility to Godalming and this contract was also awarded to the

Company. As it was almost impossible to separate the commercial and contracted portions of the Saturday service, all journeys were numbered 543 on that day.

Tillingbourne also had considerable success in gaining contracts in the West Sussex area. With a rearrangement of school transport needs, the 52 service became a Tuesdays and Fridays shopping facility between Lambs Green and Horsham via Rusper under contract to West Sussex County Council, with a change of routeing to Pondtail Road instead of North Heath Lane. Service 54 between Alfold and Plaistow was also operated under contract, whilst the Tuesdays off-peak journey of service 50 was diverted via Rowhook on behalf of the County Council. Additional off-peak journeys operated between Horsham and Walliswood, although the Horsham to Warnham circular service via Pondtail Road was withdrawn. An interesting new service operated under contract was the former Southdown route 294 between Brooks Green and Horsham, route 55, via Barns Green, Itchingfield and Christ's Hospital which was extended at peak hours to Alfold via Coolham, Billingshurst and Loxwood. Off-peak journeys on Tuesdays, Fridays and Saturdays were diverted via the Needles Estate in Horsham. A new service ran on Tuesdays, Thursdays and Saturdays, also under contract, between Horsham and Crawley via Roffey Corner, Colgate and Pease Pottage as service 56, with the Thursdays journey starting at Warnham. This replaced the non-registered facility of London Country serving Colgate and brought Tillingbourne back into the village for the first time in some years.

The increased workload of preparing for Deregulation resulted in Barry King appointing a Traffic Manager, Stephen Salmon, to replace George Burnett who had left the Company in July 1985 to join Surrey County Council. The Eastlands Garage business, owned by Tillingbourne (Metropolitan) Ltd., had been sold in late 1984, however, in September 1986, the Metropolitan Company was used to purchase premises in Horsham. It will be recalled that one Tillingbourne bus had been outstationed at Horsham Railway Yard for some years, being used by the regular Horsham driver, Mick Greenfield. The outstation vehicle was swapped over each day with the vehicle working in from Cranleigh for servicing and re-fuelling and, although this arrangement was satisfactory, there were seen to be considerable advantages in purchasing premises in Horsham, both in terms of investment and for under cover storage facilities. Consequently, from that time, the Station Yard was no longer used, the outstation vehicle being transferred to Unit 3, Foundry Close, just off Foundry Lane in Horsham.

By early 1986, the secondhand Setright ticket machines were beginning to become unreliable, and some further newer model secondhand Setright machines were purchased. In 1983 the Company had looked seriously at purchasing electronic machines, however, for a small company, the cost could not be justified in terms of the provision of better management information. Although the Setright machines acquired were in excellent condition, the opportunity arose in October 1986 to acquire secondhand Almex ticket machines, and these were used as from 20 October.

With the increased services and commitments from 26 October 1986, it is not surprising that only one vehicle was sold during that year, being the luckless Ford Transit Minibus. An interesting secondhand addition to the fleet, which brought back visual memories of the late 1970s and early 1980s was a Plaxton Derwent

**87. To maintain Surrey County Council services 547/587 in the Redhill area, Tillingbourne purchased two 21 seat Iveco minibuses in October 1986. D425 XPJ at Queensway, Redhill carries the "Hobbit" Logo. (L.James)**

bodied Leyland Leopard, ABR 778 S, whilst two new minibuses were acquired to operate the Reigate area routes, these being Robin Hood bodied Iveco Fords D 424/5 XPJ. A further secondhand purchase in 1986 was another Leyland Leopard but with a Duple Dominant Coach body, GRF 264 V. At the end of the year the fleet consisted of 20 vehicles, 17 of which had been purchased new but with the average age now four years. Nevertheless the fleet profile obviously enabled the Company to look forward to Deregulation without the worries of many other operators who were faced with the difficulties of investing in new vehicles to replace ageing fleets at a time of uncertain future profits.

There seems little doubt that the groundwork in the preparation for Deregulation was very sound. The Company was not over reliant on contracted bus services, a viable network of commercial services had been registered and was not the subject of competitive activities, while the newly acquired routes were potentially profitable and well integrated with the Company's school contract work. The geographical extremities of the Company's network were now Redhill, Crawley, Godalming and Guildford. Tillingbourne could look forward to the future with guarded but well-founded optimism.

# CHAPTER 10 - DEREGULATION AND BEYOND

The new Deregulated network commenced on Sunday, 26 October 1986 with Tillingbourne operating route 571 between Chiddingfold and Guildford, having handed over operation of the service between Guildford and Gomshall to London Country South West's route 525. The new services settled in well, and one might have been justified in thinking that the opportunities now presented to the Company would have been the most welcome challenge yet to Tillingbourne's Managing Director, Barry King. Consequently, it was a considerable surprise when it was announced that Barry King intended to leave the Company at the end of December 1986 to pursue an independent career as a consultant specialising in offering advice to both large and small bus companies. No doubt, having spent over fourteen years in building up Trevor Brown's various PSV businesses he felt that a change of direction was desirable with the opportunity of running his own company, Local Bus Consultants Ltd. which had grown out of the activities of the Tillingbourne Consultancy, a partnership formed in 1984 by Barry King and George Burnett.

During his period at the helm, Tillingbourne had grown from a very small company struggling for survival into a financially sound and substantial independent bus and coach company. In achieving this situation, the Company had acquired a definable style and a reputation out of proportion to its actual size. It had become an organisation whose activities merited the attention of the industry at large. With the departure of Barry King, Chris Bowler assumed the role of Managing Director with Stephen Salmon continuing as Traffic Manager.

Following the introduction of Deregulation there was a three month period where no changes to initial registrations were supposed to take place. Hence it was generally expected that the end of January 1987 would see very substantial changes to bus networks as it was imagined companies would move to rectify mistakes in their original registrations and introduce significant competitive services. In reality the end of January 1987 was something of an anticlimax, although Tillingbourne did make some minor changes to its network. Prior to Deregulation, Alder Valley's route 263 had terminated within the Park Mead Estate, however this had ceased following operational difficulties and complaints from some residents. Undaunted, and in the knowledge that under the new system environmental reasons for objections to bus services are no longer valid, Tillingbourne introduced diversions into the Park Mead Estate of some journeys of routes 23 and 33 as from 26 January. On a more negative note the Company deregistered route 512, operated on its behalf by Austins, due to overestimating overall revenue and the route was taken over by Dorking Coaches following retendering. In the Horsham area the Colgate to Crawley section of route 56 was reduced to a Thursdays only service. This section of the route was a commercial initiative over and above the contract requirements of West Sussex County Council. Later that year, in August, the Thursday journey was again revised to operate from Southwater.

One of the features of the post-Deregulation scene in the southern counties has been the changing fortunes of the Southdown Company. From 25 January 1987 Southdown closed its Horsham depot with a consequential withdrawal of local services. London Country South West intended to step into this vacuum with a network of minibus routes, however these could not be started until 21 February so West Sussex County Council was obliged to issue a number of short term contracts to cover local services. Most of these were awarded to London Country South West using conventional buses, however Tillingbourne operated a Saturday version of route 292 until 14 February between the centre of Horsham and the Oakhill area to the east of the town. The Southdown 570 service mentioned in Chapter 11 was transferred from Southdown to Epsom Coaches. Other changes to Tillingbourne's services in the Horsham area in 1987 were, firstly, a diversion of some route 51 journeys to operate via Foundry Lane in August. Secondly, on Mondays to Fridays, the route number of the last journey from Horsham to Cranleigh was changed from 53 to 50, operating via Broadbridge Heath. Thirdly, Tuesday and Friday off-peak journeys of route 55 were extended to Coolham and the Needles Estate diversion was withdrawn in August and, finally, a new Wednesdays only service, route 60, was started on 17 June from Horsham to Guildford via Barns Green, Billingshurst, Kirdford, Plaistow, Dunsfold, Hascombe and Godalming.

The contracted service between Farley Green and Guildford, route 545, fell due for renewal in October 1987. This time, Tillingbourne submitted an alternative quotation involving the diversion of an afternoon journey of route 25 and a morning

**88. The new Plaxton Derwent bus body was introduced to the fleet on two Bedford YMTs in March 1987. The second of the pair is D918 GRU. (P.R.Nuttall)**

peak journey from Farley Green connecting with route 25 at Albury, which was accepted by Surrey County Council. Thus, from 26 October 1987, these journeys, together with the Tuesdays and Fridays off-peak shopping journeys via Blackheath, returned to Tillingbourne after twelve months of London Country South West minibus operation. On 1 November 1987 certain journeys of the Sunday 571 service were diverted at the request of Surrey County Council to operate via Milford Hospital. At the same time it was agreed that this service should be converted to minibus operation, the latter type of vehicle being considered a more economical means of providing a Sunday service. While this was true, at certain times of the year it could create problems. On New Years Day, for example, the 571 was the only bus service between Godalming and Guildford, and with the start of the Christmas Sales, loadings could be very heavy. On one occasion, the Tillingbourne driver on duty realised that, with the numbers of passengers he had carried into Guildford in the morning, he might well be unable to cope on the return journeys. Using his initiative, he changed his minibus for a normal single deck bus at lunch time and was rewarded with capacity loads which a minibus could not have coped with at all.

During 1987 no less than four new Bedfords with the newly introduced Plaxton Derwent II bus body were purchased, D 917/8 GRU and E 215/6 MFX. By this time Bedford chassis were no longer being produced and the sale of the remaining examples at keen prices led to something of a renaissance for the make. These were the last new Bedfords to be purchased and thus marked the end of an era which had started with the purchase of LPD 12 K in 1972. Another secondhand coach arrived, this time a Leyland Tiger with Plaxton Paramount body, AEF 992 Y, which was repainted into a similar livery style to B 124 PEL. A further interesting secondhand purchase was a Bedford YMPS, B 919 NPC from Alder Valley. This unusual vehicle with a Lex Maxeta body was purchased with the Reigate area services in mind. Repainting into Tillingbourne livery was undertaken by Alder Valley, and the opportunity was taken to experiment with a change in livery style. One problem with the then current livery was that, although smart when clean, the blue sides of the bodywork showed road dirt very badly, and the new livery attempted to solve this problem by extending the yellow to cover most of the bodywork under the windows, apart from a wide blue band. This new style was approved and, as an experiment, one of the Dennis Dorchester buses was repainted accordingly, and all subsequent new single deck buses since have appeared in the new style.

The two new minibuses purchased in 1986 had been used to launch routes 547 and 587, which were marketed by Barry King as the Hobbit services. This name was chosen in reference to the mythical little characters in J R R Tolkien's books, and in a wish for originality in contrast to the inevitable "Hoppa" type of brand name. The minibuses were painted in a blue and yellow version of the Company's livery, complete with a caricature impression of a Hobbit. The services were well received by passengers who had become accustomed to an erratic service previously provided by London Country, where journeys tended to be scheduled for operation in between more important longer distance services. Tillingbourne's services were the subject of favourable comment in the local press, although one letter written by London Country's local union representative claimed that the services were bound to be better as they were heavily subsidised and the scheduling lax, conveniently ignoring the fact that network subsidy for the two previous services had been considerably higher than the new contract price! In any event the capacity of the minibuses proved to be inadequate on certain occasions, hence the requirement for the larger Bedford bus, which was normally allocated to the regular Reigate outstation driver, David Hayman. As had been the case with the Horsham operation in the past, one vehicle is regularly outstationed in the Reigate and Redhill area, being swapped on a routine basis for fuelling and maintenance purposes.

One vehicle which departed in 1987 was the first Dennis to be sold, the Lancet XTT 5 X, possibly a victim of the loss of Barry King's protection!

As in the case of 1987, 1988 was largely a year of consolidation. In May, Tillingbourne revised operations between Guidford and Cranleigh via Bramley. The decision was taken to withdraw the routeing via New Road, Wonersh and Shamley Green and to concentrate on the corridor via Birtley Road. Services 23 and 33 operated via either Run Common and Smithwood Common or via Nanhurst Corner to Cranleigh; service 23 then continued to Ewhurst, while service 33 continued to Dunsfold and Godalming via various routeings, replacing services 43 and 46. The short lived Park Mead diversion was abandoned and, on Saturdays, the 543 number was replaced by 33 in an effort to avoid confusion. In order to provide the New Road, Wonersh area with a replacement service, Surrey County Council negotiated with Tillingbourne to divert the off-peak journeys of service 545 on Tuesdays and Fridays from Blackheath via New Road, Wonersh and then to Shalford. On Thursdays the Gastonia Chauffeur Cars taxibus service 599, operating between Holmbury St.Mary and Guildford via Forest Green, Ewhurst, Cranleigh and Shalford, was also diverted to serve the New Road area.

Carlone Ltd, trading as Gastonia Chauffeur Cars, inherited the taxi and minibus operations of the Gastonia company, and was run by Martin Noakes from the Sweet Shop in Cranleigh High Street. At the time of Deregulation, Gastonia Chauffeur Cars expressed considerable interest in taking advantage of the new rules allowing licensed taxis to operate bus services, and three services were registered, all with financial support from Surrey County Council under the Deminimis provisions of the Transport Act. One of these services is mentioned above, however the other two were also replacements for former Tillingbourne journeys. On Mondays to Fridays, route 588 provided a service from Cranleigh, Ewhurst, Forest Green, Holmbury St.Mary and Abinger Hammer to Shere in the peak period, where connections were made with Tillingbourne's route 25. From 1988 the morning service was rerouted to incorporate a special schools contract and worked through to Guildford however the afternoon journey still connected at Shere with the Tillingbourne service. Route 533 provides a Fridays only facility from Cranleigh to Dorking via Forest Green and from Ranmore to Dorking, the latter replacing the special journeys of Tillingbourne route 22.

During 1987 Gastonia Chauffeur Cars moved from Cranleigh to the premises at Forest Green previously occupied by Tom Brady's Brown Motor Services next door to the erstwhile Tony McCann Motors business, and since then the company has begun to operate a number of PSV vehicles, including full size coaches.

**89. Another pair, registered E215/6 MFX, came later in 1987. The latter vehicle displays an interim updated livery with a larger area of yellow. (P.R.Nuttall)**

In May 1988 Stephen Salmon left Tillingbourne to set up his own company, Hedgerow Travel, taking with him the AEC Reliance coach, CPG 160 T which had the blue part of its livery repainted red to create a fresh identity for the new operator. Tillingbourne still undertook maintenance on the vehicle, however the Company was somewhat anxious to distance itself from the activities of its former employee, as the first move of the new company was to register a bus service, route 412, between Reigate and Redhill which competed with London Country South West. Not surprisingly, London Country South West responded to this new threat by operating additional journeys of its own services, and thus route 412 was shortlived. A school contract was obtained thereafter from Surrey County Council, and Hedgerow Travel concentrated on this activity together with private hire. As a further twist to this story, Stephen Salmon was appointed Operations Manager with London Country South West in July 1989, and CPG 160 T was then transferred to the London & Country fleet as a training vehicle!

Tillingbourne appointed John Gaff in August 1988 as the new Traffic Manager. Having been involved with the Company as a part time driver since the mid 1970s and having been primarily responsible for such matters as roadside publicity and route blinds, John Gaff was no stranger to Tillingbourne. Fortunately for the Company, little direct commercial competition had been experienced in its operating area since the start of Deregulation. The large bus companies seemed to have adopted the attitude of not attacking other operators' services provided that they were not attacked themselves. Nevertheless, there was a degree of friction from time to time as companies manouevred for position, both through alterations to their commercial operations and in tendering for local bus service contracts. In 1987 London Country had registered a rerouteing of the joint service operated with Brighton & Hove, route 773, in order to serve Shere village. This was of some concern to Tillingbourne, however the 773 was a long distance limited stop service which suffered from delays due to traffic congestion, and the level of service provided had declined with successive registration alterations. On 30 July 1988 London Country South West altered the services operated in the Dorking area. Most of these were contract services operated on behalf of Surrey County Council and thus did not affect Tillingbourne, however the 773 was withdrawn and replaced by a 90 minute frequency minibus service between Dorking and Guildford, route 473. Although less frequent than Tillingbourne's hourly 22/25 service between Gomshall, Shere and Guildford, the new service was regarded with some unease by the Company.

Consequently, Tillingbourne decided to adjust its own services to protect its position. Having obtained a new school contract, the Company felt able to register additional hourly off-peak short workings between Shere and Guildford as part of route 25, thus creating a half hourly service in the off-peak on Mondays to Fridays. In the Dorking area, service 22 was adjusted to include additional journeys to and from Westcott, thus enhancing Tillingbourne's Westcott to Dorking facility to roughly an hourly frequency. No doubt it was felt that these measures, whilst not sufficient to provoke a reaction, should act as a warning to indicate Tillingbourne's concern over what was regarded as potential encroachment.

The 547 service was altered, as from August 1988, to operate via Emlyn Road and Brambltye Park Road in Earlswood. In October, Tillingbourne ceased operation of route 571 between Chiddingfold and Guildford on Sundays as a result of Alder Valley winning the retendered contract. Finding sufficient staff to volunteer for Sunday work had not always been easy, consequently the Company had decided not to submit a tender for the new contract.

The new Traffic Manager had not been particularly happy with the renumbering of the 23/33 group of routes, which had taken place in May, as there was no indication to passengers as to the intermediate routeing of the services by reference to the route number. Consequently, as from 24 October, the services were again renumbered in an ingenious, if somewhat complex, fashion. The first digit referred to the ultimate routeing, ie "2" indicated that the service normally continued in the Ewhurst direction after Cranleigh and "4" indicated that it continued towards Godalming. The second digit indicated intermediate routeing, ie "3" meant via Smithwood Common, while "4" meant via Nanhurst Corner. Services which operated from Cranleigh to Godalming via Nanhurst Corner and Dunsfold were renumbered 46, with certain journeys extended on Mondays to Fridays to Guildford from Godalming. Thus the services were renumbered as routes 23, 24, 43, 44 and 46.

**90. On the short-lived service 60 is LCY 301X, one of five similar Lex 37 seat- bodied Bedfords acquired from both Alder Valley and Beeline. Three, including this one, were new to South Wales Transport. (P.R.Nuttall)**

**91. Displaying the new standard coach livery is E536 PRU, an example of the new Dennis Javelin chassis. It was parked at Littlemead in January 1990. (G.Burnett)**

There were two interesting new vehicle purchases in 1988. An example of the new Dennis Javelin chassis with Plaxton coachwork arrived, E 536 PRU, together with a Leyland Tiger with Plaxton Derwent II body, F 870 TLJ, similar to the Bedfords purchased the previous year. The Dennis was intended as a premium coach for private hire work, and eventually replaced the Bedford YNT, B 124 PEL. Another new chassis make for the Company was provided by the secondhand purchase of a Volvo B10M with a Plaxton Paramount coach body, A 339 HNR, whilst a further Bedford YMT with Plaxton Derwent bus body came from Felix of Stanley, Derbyshire, registered D 694 WAU. The Bedford YMP purchased secondhand from Alder Valley was considered successful and further examples were acquired from the Berks Bucks Bus Company, namely LCY 298/299/301 X (actually Bedford YMQS chassis) and B 918 NPC. The latter vehicle was involved in the disastrous fire at Newbury Garage, after purchase, and was thus received in a fire damaged condition. Consequently it was put into storage at the Company's premises at Foundry Close, Horsham and, despite considerable work to renovate it, had still not entered service by January 1990. The second Dennis Lancet bus, TTA 650 X, was sold during 1988, thus marking the demise of the 10 metre single decker from the Tillingbourne fleet. One of the AEC Reliance coaches on long term lease to Metrobus, ODV 405 W, was sold to that company following a one month period in July 1988 when it had been operated again by Tillingbourne.

In February 1988, the Tiger coach, AEF 992 Y, was re-registered with a "personal" number, TBC 658, thus following a trend among coach operators of trying to disguise the age of vehicles from their customers, particularly where expensive heavy weight machines which have a potentially long life are concerned. The Dennis Javelin coach was purchased in an all-white livery, and, as a temporary expedient, simply had the fleetnames added in blue. Some thought then went into the adoption of a more distinct coach livery, as the newly revised bus livery was similar to the existing coach style. Eventually it was decided to use a white base, with blue and yellow stripes and a large "Tillingbourne" fleetname in slanting block capitals. This style was subsequently applied to the Dennis coach, and to all coaches acquired from 1988 onwards.

It is perhaps appropriate that the final chapter in this book, taking the Tillingbourne story up to the beginning of 1990, should end on a note of interesting expansion in an unexpected area. In any event, 1989 also saw signs of a carefully planned resumption of expansion in the Company's traditional areas of operation.

The year of 1989 started with something of a shock for Tillingbourne, as it was announced that the Company had lost the contract with West Sussex County Council for the Horsham to Barns Green and Brooks Green service, route 55, to London Country South West as from 20 February. This subsequently resulted in the withdrawal, from the same day, of the commercial route 60 between Horsham and Guildford and the Company was forced to review the whole Horsham operation to assess how it might be operated in the most cost effective way.

Towards the end of 1988, a new operator appeared on the scene, Badger Buses and Coaches of Crawley, owned by a Mr Paul Gascoigne, who promptly registered a whole series of routes affecting parts of East Surrey and the Crawley/Horsham areas. Although a motley selection of vehicles was acquired, the operation was over-ambitious and was dogged with problems from the start. Badger announced

**92. The new bus livery is demonstrated by F870 TLJ, a very smart Leyland Tiger/Plaxton Derwent bus with 54 seats. (P.R.Nuttall)**

that, from 20 February, they would be operating the service between Horsham and Billingshurst on a commercial basis. Consequently, West Sussex County Council, having already tendered for a replacement service, decided not to award the contract in the light of Badger's commercially registered service. However, in January, financial problems caused the collapse of the Badger operation within a few days of the start of its bus services, and thus West Sussex County Council decided to award the contract for the Horsham to Billingshurst service to the lowest tenderer, Sussex Bus. In the meantime, Tillingbourne was searching for extra work to replace the lost Barns Green service, and the Company took the decision to operate the Horsham to Billingshurst service on a commercial basis after the Badger concern collapsed. Convinced that it had made its intentions clear to West Sussex County Council, the Company registered the appropriate services from 20 February, and was somewhat taken aback when the County Council announced that the contract had been awarded to Sussex Bus, and that this decision could not be rescinded.

Nevertheless, Tillingbourne decided to go ahead and services 57, 58 and 59 commenced operation on 20 February. Service 57 replaced the previous peak hour journeys of service 55 between Alfold and Horsham, but operating via Kirdford, Wisborough Green, Billingshurst and Slinfold, whilst service 58 was a Mondays to

Fridays operation between Horsham, Billingshurst and Parbrook. On Mondays, Wednesdays and Fridays the service was extended to Wisborough Green, and on Tuesdays and Thursdays, operating as service 59, it was extended beyond Parbrook to Adversane, Pulborough and Storrington. At the same time, alterations to service 50 resulted in additional journeys between Horsham and Warnham, diverted via Lower Broadbridge and operating via Bell Road, Dorking Road and School Hill. A new afternoon schooldays journey was operated from Horsham to Dorking via Warnham, Northlands and Kingsfold and an afternoon journey diverted between Northlands and Broadbridge Heath, via Clemsfold, to serve Farlington School. The journeys on service 51 operating via Foundry Lane were restricted to peak times only, on Mondays to Fridays, whilst service 52 was recast to operate a circular service on Tuesdays, Fridays and Saturdays from Horsham via Roffey Corner, Colgate, Faygate, Lambs Green, Rusper, Holbrook and Pondtail Road (shades of the original 451 service in the early 1970s!) with an afternoon schooldays journey from Horsham to Newdigate via Pondtail Road, Holbrook Road and Rusper. Aware of further expansion of housing in North Heath following the opening of the Horsham By-Pass in that area, Tillingbourne was anxious to stamp its presence there as early as possible, hence new service 61 also commenced on 20 February operating on an hourly frequency from Horsham via Station, Pondtail Road, Holbrook, North Heath Lane and Blackhorse Way mainly using the same vehicle which provided the extra Warnham journeys on service 50. Finally in the Horsham area, service 56 was recast to operate two return journeys on Thursdays only between Horsham and Crawley, one via Colgate and Pease Pottage and the other via Faygate.

In the Cranleigh area, the Company had a minor success in taking over the morning peak hour service from Loxwood to Cranleigh previously operated by Alder Valley under contract to West Sussex County Council as the last remnant of route 269. As West Sussex decided the service was no longer required from Plaistow and Ifold, responsibility was transferred to Surrey County Council, who felt that a suitable Deminimis agrement was the best answer in order to retain all journeys on that routeing with the one operator. The new journey was, naturally, operated as service 44. For some years there had been a gap in service provision between Ewhurst and Cranleigh in the morning peak by both Tillingbourne and Alder Valley, which affected children attending Glebelands School in Cranleigh. In an attempt to solve this problem, Surrey County Council suggested to Tillingbourne that the school contract from the Ewhurst area to Glebelands school should be operated as a local bus service, and this was duly registered as route 33 in February. Later that year in September, it was extended to start at Coverwood Corner.

Tillingbourne found itself in continuous competition with the subsidised Sussex Bus services between Horsham and Billingshurst and, not surprisingly, there was insufficient revenue to sustain both operations. With no likelihood of Sussex Bus withdrawing their services, Tillingbourne felt obliged to de-register routes 57, 58 and 59, which ceased to operate after 28 April 1989. As the services were operated separately, there was no direct impact on the Company's other services in the Horsham area. For some time British Aerospace had been running down its factory at Weybridge, and staff were being redeployed to other plants, notably that at

Dunsfold Aerodrome. British Aerospace approached Tillingbourne regarding the possibility of the Company operating a subsidised peak hours facility from Guildford Station to Dunsfold, and this commenced on 31 July 1989 as route 45, via Bramley and Grafham.

Further changes to Tillingbourne's services in the Surrey area from 28 October

**93. Acquired from Woodstones Coaches of Kidderminster in August 1988 was A339 HNR, the first Volvo in the fleet. (G.Burnett)**

1989 resulted in an expansion into an area hitherto unserved by the Company. It may be recalled that, some years previously, Barry King had tried to persuade Surrey County Council that Tillingbourne could assist in providing a better bus service for the village of Puttenham. That offer had not been taken up, and eventually the Puttenham Village service had passed to Blue Saloon as contracted service 565. Usage of the Mondays to Fridays off-peak service to Guildford had not been encouraging, however an experimental service on Mondays and Thursdays from Puttenham to Farnham had fared better. The County Council considered that a twice a week facility between Puttenham and Guildford would be adequate to meet needs, and thus when the contract fell due for renewal, the 565 route then became a Mondays and Thursdays service from Godalming to Farnham via Farncombe, Puttenham, Seale and the Sands which was awarded to Alder Valley. Successful negotiations were concluded with Tillingbourne to rearrange the 545 Farley Green service to operate on Tuesdays and Fridays only between Farley Green and the Sands via Blackheath, Wonersh (New Road), Shalford, Guildford, Royal County

**94. Similar in appearance to F870 TLJ, but this time on Bedford chassis, D694 WAU calls at Shere. This almost new secondhand purchase came from the well-known Felix of Stanley. (L.James)**

**95. The most recent full-size purchase has been G401 DPD, a magnificent Plaxton-bodied Scania K93. Posed at Smithwood Common, its capacity is 57 seated plus 24 standing, and it is the first and so far the only 12 metre length vehicle owned. (G.Burnett)**

Hospital, Fairlands Estate, Normandy, Wyke, Christmaspie, Wanborough, Puttenham and Seale, with some journeys operating direct via the Hogs Back. This has proven to be successful, with usage and revenue improving considerably as a result.

Arrangements were also made to change certain Saturday 43, 44 and 46 journeys to improve the Cranleigh to Godalming service with the result that the previous 543 contract has been altered to a Deminimis agreement between Tillingbourne and Surrey County Council. Dunsfold, Hascombe and Busbridge have thus gained an off-peak service to both Godalming and Guildford as from 28 October, with the only side effect being the off-peak Saturday route 50 journey having to commence from Walliswood instead of Cranleigh. From the same date, all journeys from Cranleigh terminating in Godalming were extended to operate via Catteshall Lane to Farncombe.

However, the most unexpected news of 1989 was the announcement in early November that the Company had been successful in tendering for a substantial number of routes put out to re-tender by Hampshire County Council in the Blackwater Valley area. Previously Tillingbourne had always looked to Surrey and West Sussex for expansion, apart from the venture in the Orpington area in the early 1980s, although the Company had expressed interest in the town services in Alton when these had been re-tendered by Hampshire County Council. The new contracts obtained represented approximately half of the total tendered by Hampshire in the Blackwater Valley, and were primarily for minibus services in the Fleet and Farnborough areas. Tillingbourne had to prepare for the operation of this new network with some urgency, and the management was soon involved in the business of finding suitable premises, purchasing new vehicles, employing staff and preparing timetables and schedules. The number of operating licences held by the Company had gradually risen to 24 (some of which were in the name of the Sussex and Metropolitan subsidiaries), and a further 6 licences were requested and obtained with the intention of eventually being transferred to a new subsidiary, predictably called Tillingbourne (Hampshire) Ltd.

The Hampshire operation requires a minimum of six vehicles on an all day basis, operating a total of 11 routes. It was decided to operate these services under the "Hobbit" marketing name, and an integrated re-numbering scheme was implemented. Previously, the route numbers for these services, all of which had been operated by Alder Valley, were either in the old, pre-Deregulation, "400" series, or in a two digit series introduced for both commercial and contract services in October 1986. Tillingbourne decided to adopt a two digit system, prefixed by "F" which could be taken to mean either Fleet or Farnborough. Thus routes such as 25 or 26 became F25 and F26, and routes such as 412 or 436 became F12 and F36 respectively. The Monday to Saturday services gained were F13, Farnborough to Quetta Park via Cove, Fleet and Crookham, F14, Fleet to Crookham (The Verne) via Humphrey Park or Crookham Village, F15/F16, Fleet circulars via Pondtail and either Velmead Road or Aldershot Road, F17, Farnborough to Fleet via Cove and Ancells Farm, F25, Farnborough to Pyestock Estate, F26, Farnborough to Farnborough Street and the Ship Inn, F36, Farnborough to Guillemont Fields via Cove and Minley Estate and F37, Farnborough to Rafborough. Additionally, two Monday to Friday peak hour services were gained, F12, Crookham (The Verne) to

Aldershot via Fleet, Cove, Farnborough and North Camp, and F38, Yateley to Fleet Station via Vigo Lane.

**96. G407 DPD is a coach-seated Iveco with Carlyle bodywork. Seen in the photograph (left to right) are Trevor Brown, proprietor; John Gaff, Traffic Manager and Chris Bowler, Managing Director. (G.Burnett)**

The new network commenced operation on 2 January 1990, and the Company has committed itself to maintaining the highest quality of service. Temporary premises were used adjacent to the Farnham Coaches depot in Odiham Road, Folly Hill, although it is the intention to acquire more suitable facilities as soon as possible. In view of the extent of the services concerned, the distance from Cranleigh and the establishment of an outstation, it will be fascinating to see how successful this operation becomes and what systems are implemented to ensure effective management. Past experience augurs well in this respect.

As far as acquiring full size vehicles is concerned, 1989 might be described as a Scandanavian year. A further secondhand Volvo B10M coach was purchased from Victoria Motorways, Treorchy with a Plaxton Supreme V body, NUH 262 X. After repainting into the new Tillingbourne coach livery, the vehicle was given the "personal" registration number 508 AHU. A more interesting new purchase was

**97. The award of new contracts for services in Farnborough and Fleet in Hampshire prompted the arrival of five Iveco/Carlyle minibuses. G406 DPD on its first day in service was on route F37 at Kingsmead, Farnborough. ((L.James)**

**98. A close-up view of the caricature figure of a Tolkien "Hobbit" now displayed on minibuses D424/5 XPJ, G402-6 DPD and G810 DPH. (G.Burnett)**

that of a Scania K93 rear engined bus with Plaxton Derwent body. This vehicle is only the second rear engined bus ever owned, the first being a Daimler Roadliner in the 1970s, but is also the first of 12 metre length in the fleet. Purchased in October 1989 in an all-white livery, it was stored at the Company's premises in Horsham prior to entering service in full fleet livery in December 1989. This impressive vehicle seats 57 passengers, with room for 24 standees, thus being capable of carrying a total of 81 people.

The first Bedford YMT with Plaxton Bustler body, FOD 941 Y, was sold in 1989, and all the small Bedfords acquired from the Berks Bucks Bus Company had been disposed of by the end of the year, with the exception of B 918 NPC, which was still being refurbished by the Company. The chosen minibus type for the new Hampshire services is, again, the Iveco 49.10, and a total of six new ones were taken into stock. The first to arrive in November 1989 was G 407 DPD, a dual purpose bodied version with a Carlyle body seating 25, whilst the balance of five, G 402-6 GPD arrived in December with standard Carlyle 25 seat bus bodies, incorporating a double seat which folds to create extra luggage capacity. Whilst the coach seated vehicle remained at Cranleigh, the two original 21 seat vehicles were repainted into the new livery, complete with white roofs, and were transferred to the Hampshire operation to make up the seven vehicles, including one spare, needed to operate the services.

In some ways history now seems to have gone full circle. Whilst the relatively new management team is vigourously pursuing the policies which proved so successful in the late 1970s and early 1980s, the principal architect of those policies, Barry King, was appointed, in September 1989, Commercial Manager (West) of London & Country, the new trading name of London Country Bus (South West) Ltd, thus returning to the Reigate based Company after a gap of eighteen years. As bus companies, both large and small, struggle to take up the challenges of providing attractive services and securing an acceptable return on capital invested, all within the competitive environment, it would be not only difficult, but also foolish, to make predictions as to which will survive and prosper and which will fall by the wayside. In 1974, in "The Story of 50 years of Independent Bus Operation in West Surrey", Barry King concluded by stating that it would be, "false to look ahead with glowing optimism to Tillingbourne's centenary in fifty years' time." Nevertheless, sixteen years later, Tillingbourne is an almost unrecognisable concern. The vehicle fleet has been upgraded to a standard where it is probably the most modern in the south east of England, secure tenure of suitable premises in Cranleigh have been obtained, along with ownership of premises in Horsham, the size of the fleet has expanded threefold and the operating territory has grown to reach Fleet in the west and Redhill in the east.

There are uncertain times in the bus operating industry at the dawn of the 1990s, and in the last few years many famous independent names have succumbed to take over bids from a new set of ever expanding conglomerates. It is to be hoped that Tillingbourne will be able to continue its proud record of independence and that the livery of yellow ochre and Danube blue will still be a familiar sight in Surrey, Sussex and even Hampshire in the years to come. Who knows, perhaps a future historian will be able to sit down in the year 2024 and write an updated history of the Company's first one hundred years after all!

## Tillingbourne Hampshire Services
January 1990

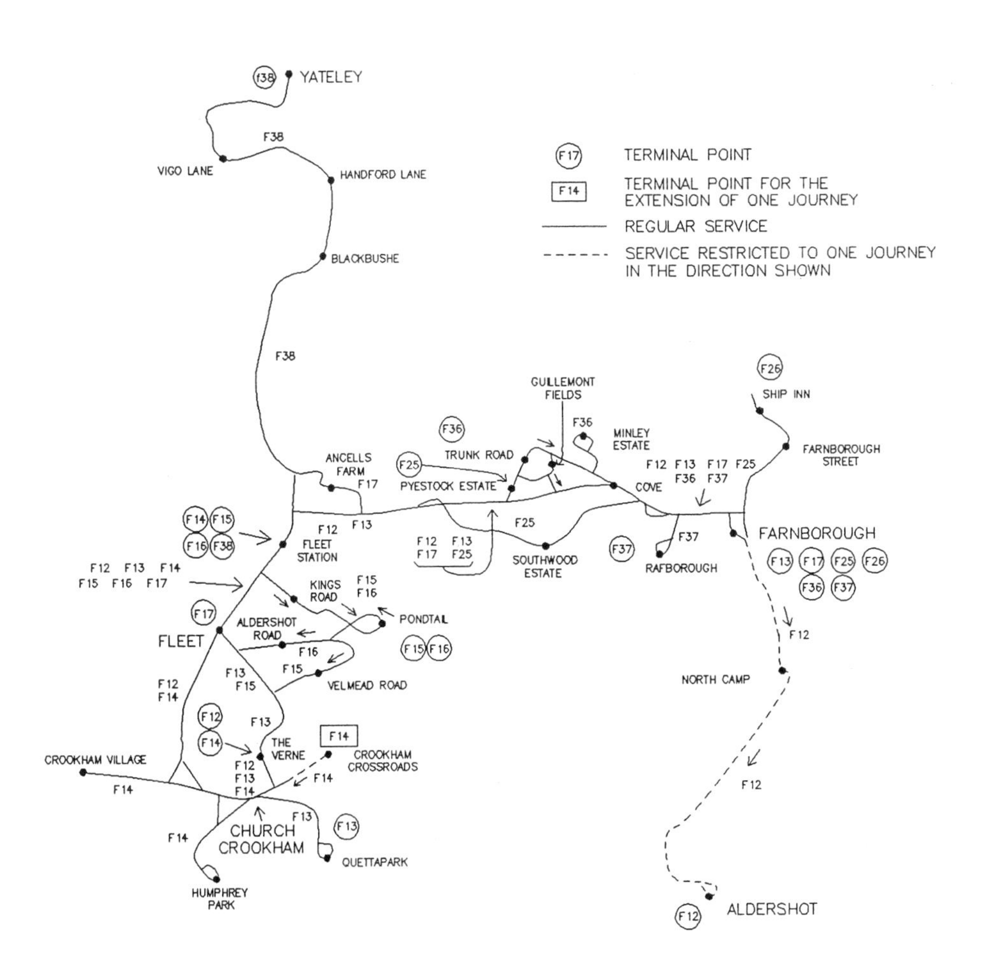

# POST SCRIPT

It is hoped that readers will have gained an impression from this history of how the Tillingbourne Bus Company has grown and developed over the years. Unfortunately, it is difficult in such an account to convey the real ethos of the company, which consists of much more than simply the livery style, the routes operated or the vehicles owned. All bus companies have an indefinable style of their own, which owes something to their history, to their work practices and to those employed, but often seems able to continue over the years regardless of changes in management and the steady turnover of staff.

Perhaps the spirit of the Company can best be encapsulated in its everyday activities and organisation, as seen from the perspective of the Traffic Manager in the early 1980s.

Arriving at the Cranleigh Depot at about 0700 hrs on a weekday, buses would be seen to be parked in two neat rows, with two or three parked sideways at the front, all having been fuelled the previous evening. At that time, the first driver should have been about to depart (services start earlier now) and the rest of the drivers would arrive between 0700 hrs and 0730 hrs. Climbing the flight of steps to the office area, two or three drivers would be seen collecting their Setright ticket machines, which would have been prepared by the Traffic Manager the previous day, and checking their vehicle allocation. Nowadays the staff are issued with a complete uniform, including Tillingbourne tie, but at that time the only piece of uniform supplied was a bright blue jacket, which drivers jokingly claimed qualified them as ice cream salesmen! Having swept out their own vehicles and checked the oil and water levels, there was usually time for them to have a cup of tea and a chat, which all added to the feeling of camaraderie, at least until the time when the Traffic Manager (gently), or the Chief Engineer (less gently!) would remind them that it was time to leave.

Rosters were designed to allow a twelve week cycle for each driver, including coverage for staff absent for entitled holidays, however, in cases of of sickness, either one of the engineering staff, or the Traffic Manager, would have to cover, depending on the pressure of work at the time. In any event, it was normal practice for the Traffic Manager to drive a school contract. The Managing Director would arrive at about 0800 hrs, and, on the occasions of staff sickness, either he or the Chief Engineer would operate the last school contract to leave the yard. Of course, all this was more excitingon snowy days, with uncertainty about whether the Ewhurst to Peaslake road would be passable, as it was seldom dealt with by the local authority. These weather conditions would result in heroic efforts to start reluctant buses, most of which were left outside each night, and hurried discussions over the most suitable vehicle allocation. It was well known that manual gearchanges were best in these conditions, and vehicles equipped with air operated throttles highly suspect! Of all the vehicles operated at that time, Leyland Leopards and Tigers were the ones to avoid in the ice and snow.

Apart from the Managing Director and one of the engineering staff, the Depot was virtually deserted until just after 0900 hrs, when the school contract vehicles would begin to return. Engineering staff would then begin their day's planned work, which could include bodywork repairs, routine maintenance, general repairs and preparation for annual tests. Standards under Chris Bowler have always been of the highest, and the Company strove to ensure that no vehicle ever failed its annual inspection at the Slyfield Green Testing Station. Immediately after 0900 hrs, Barry King would always count the previous day's takings, which normally took just under an hour, although as the years passed with increased expansion, this job became more onerous, particularly for the Traffic Manager, who often had to carry all the takings to the local bank!

Events during the day were many and varied, and often unpredictable, particularly if an accident caused a road closure, or road works played havoc with the schedules. Generally, the buses operating local services did not return to the Depot until the early evening, all meal breaks being scheduled to take place at Guildford Bus Station. Although checks were carried out on the correct operation of the services, particularly if one of the management was driving, staff were given a high degree of responsibility, and the majority responded well to this trust. Morale was almost always high among the Company's staff, no doubt encouraged by having a modern fleet with the regular arrival of brand new vehicles. Guildford Bus Station has a staff canteen, frequented by the drivers of all the companies, and it was often amusing to listen to the talk there, which, as always with bus operating staff, seemed to consist of spreading rumours, telling jokes and stories and endeavouring to "wind up" staff from other companies. It has to be said that Tillingbourne had its share of drivers who delighted in these activities. A more important characteristic of the staff was their relationship with their customers, which was usually excellent. Two incidents which come to mind demonstrate this. Once, a certain driver arrived at work in an unfamiliar elderly, but sound, car, which it transpired had been donated to him by a lady who used the bus service regularly, but was no longer able to drive. On another occasion, Tony Fustes was presented with a copy of Cervantes' "Don Quixote" in Spanish by an elderly lady from the Forest Green area, who had struck up a friendship with him. When this lady was housebound through illness, Tony arranged to do her shopping for her during his meal break, and delivered the groceries to her doorstep on his next run to Forest Green. Such incidents are often recorded in the rural areas of England, but are probably far rarer in the Home Counties adjoining London. Good relations also existed with many of the local village traders, for example Sam Errett's Butchers Shop in Peaslake, as well as producing some of the finest sausages in the south east of England, was a vital communication point for Tillingbourne drivers, who were able to ask Sam to pass on messages to Cranleigh about road conditions and unexpected delays.

All members of the management drove regularly, and this resulted in a more direct relationship between management and both staff and passengers than is possible in a larger company. Any member of staff could gain easy access to the Managing Director, Chief Engineer or Traffic Manager should he wish to discuss any problems, and, from time to time, there would be staff meetings in the early evening, after the day's work, when all sorts of matters could be discussed with frankness on both sides. After the days at Gomshall, everyone's life was made easier by having such suitable premises, which although simple, provided a staff mess room, offices for management, a clothing and equipment storeroom and a large washroom which included a shower facility, particularly popular with staff on a Saturday evening prior to a night out and after a hard day's driving!

Whilst conditions and wage rates were not dissimilar to other companies in the area, there were certain individualities with the Tillingbourne Company, in particular the fact that most weekly shifts consisted of four and a half day periods and that commission was paid on the daily cash takings.

Up until 1985, the day's work at Tillingbourne usually ended soon after the last bus arrived in at 1835 hrs. Vehicles would be fuelled and parked, and, after checking that all buses were serviceable for the next day and listening to any stories of the day's events which the drivers may have had to tell, the premises would be locked and left ready for the following morning. Although there may well have been frustrations and worries from time to time, the majority of former employees undoubtedly have, as an abiding memory of their period of employment with the Company, the good comradeship and the sheer joy to be derived from driving in the early morning on a bright and sunny day through the villages and along the beautiful Tillingbourne Valley.

## An Appreciation of the 8.13 (1940 - 1944)

From fair Peaslake, set in Surrey,
Where the views are wondrous fine,
Do some workers, young and ancient,
Into Guildford get by nine.

Faithful Tilly! Big or little,
Steered by Jack or Bert to town,
Red and grey bus, crammed with people,
Over lovely Merrow Down.

Does some worker's clock betray her,
And she wildly fears she's late,
Rushes out of doors so quickly,
Finds the bus beside her gate.

Faithful Tilly! Jack still smiling,
Never passes by a place,
Where he knows each morning early,
There should be a well-known face.

Is the weather dark and stormy?
Does the snow come whirling down.
Icy roads prove traps for buses,
Skid marks strow the road's white crown.

Faithful Tilly! Crowded, weighted,
Still sails safely, swiftly on,
Guided by her clever drivers,
And the race to town is won.

When the gate man, at the crossing,
Clears the way for Tilly's load,
Jack, in passing, shows green buses,
How he steers, yet keeps the road.

Faithful Tilly! Always willing,
Cannot let her workers down,
Keeps on slipping, sliding, skidding,
Passing buses green and brown.

Now the morning's getting lighter,
And the sun begins to shine,
And the weather, turning warmer,
Spring is coming - it's a sign.

Faithful Tilly! How we thank you,
And your drivers Jack and Bert;
All the journeys done so safely,
Without bruises, scratch or hurt.

Many journeys may you travel,
Up and down the Peaslake hill;
Grateful workers you are serving
With your trusty engine still.

Faithful Tilly! Valued helper,
We can only tell you so,
But we know you will believe us,
As we always with you go.

# APPENDIX 1

# LIST OF ROUTES

## A. Routes Primarily in Surrey Operated by Tillingbourne Bus Co. Ltd.

### 1. Guildford - Cranleigh via Newlands Corner, Peaslake and Ewhurst - Routes 448/449

| | | |
|---|---|---|
| - | 1924 | New daily service: Guildford - Merrow - Newlands Corner - Silent Pool - Shere - Gomshall. |
| - | 1925 | Extended from Gomshall to Peaslake. |
| - | 12/8/64 | Extended Mondays to Saturdays from Peaslake to Ewhurst. Tillingbourne acquired journeys previously operated by London Transport as Service 448. |
| - | 28/11/65 | Peaslake - Ewhurst section withdrawn. |
| 448 | 4/71 | Tillingbourne numbered service as Route 448. |
| 448 | 16/7/72 | Sunday Service withdrawn. |
| 449 | 21/6/73 | Two 448 journeys on Thursdays renumbered 449 and extended from Peaslake to Ewhurst - Ewhurst Green |
| - | | Walliswood - Oakwoodhill - Ockley - Capel - Kingsfold - Warnham - Broadbridge Heath - Horsham. |
| 449 | 12/7/73 | Service 449 withdrawn. |
| 448 | 3/5/76 | Service 448 extended Mondays to Saturdays from Peaslake to Ewhurst and Cranleigh. One schoolday journey each way extended from Ewhurst to Ewhurst Green - Ellens Green - Rudgwick - Bucks Green - The Haven. |
| 448 | 7/77 | Journeys to The Haven withdrawn. |
| 448 | 5/78 | "Scenic Circular" Summer Sunday and Bank Holiday service: operated until 9/78 Guildford - Cranleigh via normal route and then Nanhurst Corner - Hascombe - Winkworth Arboretum - Godalming - Farncombe - Peasmarsh - Guildford. |
| 448 | 5/79 | "Scenic Circular" re-introduced until 9/79. Diverted between Nanhurst Corner and Hascombe via Alfold Crossways and Dunsfold. |
| 448 | 12/4/85 | Service 448 withdrawn and replaced by services 23, 25 and 44.(q.v.) |

### 2. Guildford - Farley Green via Shalford, Chilworth and Albury - Routes 450, 445, 447 and 545

| | | |
|---|---|---|
| - | 1924 | New daily service: Guildford - Shalford - Chilworth - Albury - Park Gates. |
| - | 1926 | Extended on Tuesdays, Fridays and Saturdays from Park Gates to Little London, Brook and Farley Green. Also additional journeys on Tuesdays, Fridays and Saturdays: Guildford - Shalford - Chilworth - Blackheath. |
| - | 1929 | Blackheath journeys withdrawn. Route became daily operation Guildford - Farley Green. |
| - | c1950-54 | Extended from Farley Green to Treetops Holiday Camp (request only). Soon withdrawn. |
| 450 | 4/71 | Tillingbourne numbered service as Route 450. |
| 450 | 23/10/71 | Sunday service withdrawn. |
| 450 | 19/6/72 | Certain journeys operated between Park Gates and Farley Green direct via Brook Crossing. |
| 450 | 7/1/74 | One journey each way diverted at Chilworth to double-run to Blackheath. |
| 445 | 31/8/80 | Service 450 re-numbered 445. |
| 445 | 13/8/81 | Blackheath diversion withdrawn on Saturdays. New service 447 |
| 447 | | on Thursdays: Guildford - Shalford - Chilworth - Albury - Park Gates - Brook - Farley Green - Shamley Green - Cranleigh. |
| 445 | 5/7/82 | Service 447 withdrawn. Some journeys on 445 diverted at |
| 447 | | Park Gates to Silent Pool and Shere. Blackheath diversion reduced to Thursdays only. Monday - Friday garage journey extended from Park Gates to Shere Heath - Peaslake - Ewhurst - Cranleigh. |

| | | |
|---|---|---|
| 445 | 1/11/82 | Shere journeys replaced by service 446 (q.v.) and Cranleigh garage journey withdrawn. |
| 445 | 12/4/85 | Service 445 withdrawn and replaced by service 25.(q.v.) |
| 545 | 26/10/87 | New Tuesday and Friday service operated under contract to Surrey C.C.: Guildford - Shalford - Chilworth - Blackheath - Albury - Albury Heath - Little London - Farley Green. Also schoolday journey: Tillingbourne School - Chilworth - Albury - Farley Green. |
| 545 | 17/5/88 | Most Tuesday and Friday journeys diverted between Shalford and Chilworth Station via Wonersh - Barnett Lane - Blackheath. |
| 545 | 30/10/89 | Revised to operate Tuesdays and Fridays only. All journeys via Wonersh and Blackheath. Extended from Guildford to Royal Surrey County Hospital - Fairlands Estate - Normandy - Wyke - Wanborough -Puttenham - Seale - Sands. Some journeys direct between Royal Surrey County Hospital and Puttenham via Hogs Back. |

### 3.Guildford Local Services - Warren Road and Pewley Way - Route 451

| | | |
|---|---|---|
| - | 12/29 | New daily service: Guildford - St.Luke's Hospital - Warren Road. |
| - | 12/8/64 | Tillingbourne took over Monday - Saturday London Transport service 448A: Guildford - Pewley Way. |
| - | 27/11/65 | Pewley Way service withdrawn. |
| 451 | 4/71 | Tilingbourne numbered Warren Road service as route 451. |
| 451 | 16/10/71 | Service 451 withdrawn. |

### 4.Guildford - Cranleigh via Chilworth, Gomshall, Holmbury St.Mary, Westcott, Dorking, Brockham, Leigh and Newdigate - Routes 22, 444, 453 and 512

| | | |
|---|---|---|
| - | 8/29 | New daily service: Gomshall - Abinger Hammer - Wotton Hatch - Westcott - Dorking. Later extended from Gomshall to Peaslake. |
| - | 11/29 | Peaslake to Dorking service withdrawn. |
| 453 | 5/4/77 | New Tuesday service 453: Cranleigh - Ewhurst - Forest Green - Ockley - Capel - Newdigate - Park Gate - Gadbrook - Strood Green - Brockham Green - Kiln Lane - Reigate - Coulsdon - Purley - West Croydon. |
| 453 | 27/9/77 | Service 453 withdrawn. |
| 444 | 12/11/81 | New Thursday service 444: Cranleigh - Shamley Green - Wonersh - Bramley - Shalford - Chilworth - Albury - Shere - Gomshall - Abinger Hammer - Wotton Hatch - Westcott - Croydon. |
| 444 | 4/2/82 | Service 444 withdrawn. |
| 444 | 1/11/82 | New Thursday service: Ockley - Oakwoodhill - Walliswood - Mayes Green - Forest Green - Ewhurst - Cranleigh. Also schoolday journeys between Cranleigh and Dorking via Oakwoodhill and Ockley or Ewhurst and Forest Green. |
| 444 | 24/2/83 | Thursday service withdrawn. |
| 444 | 14/4/85 | Schoolday journeys withdrawn. |
| 22 | 14/4/85 | New Monday to Saturday service ("The Villager"): Shere - Gomshall - Abinger Hammer - Sutton - Holmbury St. Mary - Abinger Common - Wotton - Westcott - Dorking. Extended on Fridays from Dorking to Ranmore. Diverted Monday to Friday at Holmbury St.Mary to serve Forest Green replacing service 446.(q.v.) Schoolday journeys diverted between Abinger Common and Dorking via Friday Street and Broadmoor. On Saturdays, journeys commenced at Guildford and ran to Shere and Dorking via Shalford - Chilworth - Albury - Silent Pool. |
| 512 | 27/10/86 | New school day service operated as route 512 under contract to Surrey C.C.: Ockley - Forest Green - Holmbury St.Mary - Sutton - Holmbury St.Mary - Abinger Common - Wotton - Westcott - Dorking - Sondes Place School. (Sub-contracted to Austins Coaches). |
| 22 | 27/10/86 | Revised to operate Guildford - Dorking (Monday to Saturday) and extended from Dorking to Brockham Lane - Brockham Green - Strood Green - Leigh - Park Gate - Newdigate. Peak hour journeys continue from Newdigate to Beare Green - Ockley - Forest Green - Ewhurst - Cranleigh. Forest Green off-peak diversion and Ranmore section withdrawn. Schoolday Broadmoor journeys withdrawn. |

| | | |
|---|---|---|
| 512 | 26/1/87 | Service 512 withdrawn. |

### 5. Guildford - Horsham via Chilworth, Abinger Hammer and Forest Green - Route 446

| | | |
|---|---|---|
| 446 | 1/11/82 | New Monday to Saturday service: Guildford - Shalford - Chilworth - Albury - Silent Pool - Shere - Gomshall - Abinger Hammer - Sutton - Holmbury St.Mary - Forest Green - Ewhurst - Ewhurst Green - Walliswood - Oakwoodhill. Then via Ockley and Kennels Crossroads or Broadstone Corner and Rowhook to Northlands - Warnham -Broadbridge Heath - Horsham. Also garage journeys from Cranleigh to Guildford and Horsham via Ewhurst. |
| 446 | 6/6/83 | Service curtailed to operate between Guildford and ForestGreen, with peak hour journeys through to Ewhurst and Cranleigh. Saturday journeys extended from Forest Green to Horsham via Mayes Green - Walliswood - Oakwoodhill. |
| 446 | 10/7/83 | Summer Sunday and Bank Holiday service operated by a vintage bus between Guildford and Gomshall until 25/9/83. |
| 446 | 12/4/85 | Service 446 withdrawn and replaced by services 22 and 25 (q.v.) |

### 6. Guildford - Cranleigh/Godalming via either Peaslake or Bramley. - Routes 23, 24, 25, 33, 43, 44, 45, 46 and 543

| | | |
|---|---|---|
| 23 | 13/4/85 | New service operated as route 23: Guildford - Shalford - Bramley - Wonersh - New Road - Shamley Green - Gaston Gate. Then via Rowly or Smithwood Common to Cranleigh - Ewhurst (Monday to Saturday). |
| 25 | 13/4/85 | New service operated as route 25 to replace routes 445 and 448: Guildford - Shalford - Chilworth - Albury - Silent Pool - Shere - Gomshall (Daily) - Peaslake - Ewhurst - Cranleigh (Monday to Saturday). Some Monday to Friday journeys diverted between Albury and Shere/Peaslake via Albury Heath - Brook - Farley Green - Little London - Shere Heath. Friday shoppers bus: Ockley - Oakwoodhill - Walliswood - Ewhurst Green - Ewhurst - Peaslake - Shere Heath - Little London - Farley Green - Brook - Albury Heath - Albury - Blackheath - Chilworth - Shalford - Guildford. |
| 33 | 13/4/85 | New service operated as route 33: Guildford - Shalford - Bramley - Birtley - Grafham - Palmers Cross - Leathern Bottle - Nanhurst Corner - West Cranleigh - Cranleigh (Daily). Extended from Cranleigh to Ewhurst on Sundays. On Saturdays ran from Guildford to West Cranleigh only. |
| 44 | 13/4/85 | New service operated as route 44 to replace certain Monday to Friday peak hour journeys of route 448: Cranleigh - Ewhurst - Peaslake - Gomshall - Shere - Silent Pool - Newlands Corner - Merrow - Guildford. |
| 33 | 24/3/86 | Some service 33 journeys diverted via Elmbridge RHA. |
| 23 | 27/10/86 | All service 23 journeys diverted to operate via Smithwood Common instead of Rowly. |
| 25 | 27/10/86 | Friday Ockley journey, Farley Green journeys and Sunday service of route 25 withdrawn. |
| 33 | 27/10/86 | Service 33 revised to operate Guildford to Ewhurst (Monday to Saturday). |
| 44 | 27/10/86 | Monday to Friday peak hour journeys operated as route 44 re-numbered to operate as route 25. |
| 43 | 27/10/86 | New service operated as route 43: Cranleigh - Hazelwood - Alfold Crossways - Alfold - Loxwood - Ifold - Plaistow - Durfold Wood - Dunsfold - Loxhill - Hascombe - Winkworth - Busbridge - Godalming (Monday to Friday). |
| 46 | 27/10/86 | New service operated as route 46: Cranleigh - Nanhurst Corner - Dunsfold - Loxhill - Hascombe - Winkworth - Busbridge - Godalming (Monday to Friday). |
| 543 | 27/10/86 | New service partly operated under contract to Surrey C.C. on Saturday only following route of 43/46. |
| 23 | 26/1/87 | Some journeys of routes 23 and 33 diverted via Park Mead |
| 33 | | Estate between Cranleigh and Ewhurst. |
| 25 | 26/10/87 | One Monday to Friday journey each way of route 25 diverted to serve Farley Green. |
| 23 | 16/5/88 | Service 23 diverted to operate between Bramley and Cranleigh via Birtley - Run Common - Gaston Gate - Smithwood Common or via Grafham - Palmers Cross - Leathern Bottle - Nanhurst Corner. Parkmead diversion withdrawn. |
| 33 | 16/5/88 | Service 33 revised to operate as service 23 between Guildford and Cranleigh, then via Hazelwood - Alfold Crossways - Alfold - Loxwood - Ifold - Plaistow - Durfold Wood or via Nanhurst Corner to Dunsfold - Loxhill - Hascombe - Winkworth - Busbridge - Godalming (Monday to Saturday). |
| 43 | 16/5/88 | Services 43, 46 and 543 withdrawn and replaced by service 33. |

| | | |
|---|---|---|
| 24 | 24/10/88 | All service 23 journeys operating via Nanhurst Corner re-numbered as route 24. |
| 33 | 24/10/88 | Service 33 withdrawn and replaced by routes 43, 44 and 46. |
| 43 | 24/10/88 | New service replacing certain route 33 journeys, same routeing between Guildford and Cranleigh as route 23, then via Loxwood - Plaistow - Dunsfold (Monday to Saturday) and Godalming (Monday to Friday). |
| 44 | 24/10/88 | New service replacing certain route 33 journeys, same routeing between Guildford and Cranleigh as route 24, then via Loxwood - Plaistow - Dunsfold - Godalming (Monday to Saturday). |
| 46 | 24/10/88 | New service replacing certain route 33 journeys: Cranleigh - Nanhurst Corner - Dunsfold - Loxhill - Hascombe - Winkworth - Busbridge - Godalmimg (Monday to Saturday) - Farncombe - Peasmarsh - Guildford (Monday to Friday). Certain journeys diverted at Alfold Crossways to operate direct to Dunsfold. |
| 33 | 20/2/89 | New service operating on schooldays: Duke of Kent School - Ewhurst - Ewhurst Green - Ellens Green - Cox Green - Baynards - Hazelwood - Cranleigh (Glebelands School). |
| 44 | 20/2/89 | Additional Monday to Friday morning peak hour journey on service 44: Loxwood - Alfold - Alfold Crossways - Nanhurst Corner - Cranleigh (replacing Alder Valley 269). |
| 45 | 31/7/89 | New service, Monday to Friday, peak hour works service: Guildford Station - Shalford - Bramley - Birtley - Grafham - Palmers Cross - Dunsfold (BAe Works). |
| 33 | 4/9/89 | Service 33 journeys extended back to start at Coverwood Corner. |
| 43 | 28/10/89 | Journeys of routes 43 and 44 terminating in Godalming |
| 44 | | extended via Catteshall Lane to Farncombe. |
| 46 | 28/10/89 | Service 46 on Saturdays extended from Godalming to Farncombe - Peasmarsh - Guildford. Journeys terminating in Godalming extended via Catteshall Lane to Farncombe. |

## 7. Wisborough Green - Cranleigh. - Routes 452 and 453

| | | |
|---|---|---|
| 452 | 7/2/75 | New service operating on Fridays: Wisborough Green - New Pound - Roundstreet Common - Loxwood - Alfold - Alfold Crossways - Hazelwood - Cranleigh. |
| 452 | 8/8/75 | Service 452 diverted between Wisborough Green and Loxwood via Kirdford - Mackerel Common - Plaistow - Ifold. |
| 452 | 2/1/79 | Wisborough Green - Plaistow section only operated during school holidays. |
| 453 | 24/9/79 | Service 452 re-numbered as route 453. |
| 453 | 29/8/80 | Service 453 withdrawn. |

## 8. Guildford - Godalming - Milford - Witley - Chiddingfold - Route 571

| | | |
|---|---|---|
| 571 | 26/10/86 | New Sunday and Bank Holiday service operated under contract to Surrey C.C.: Guildford - Peasmarsh - Farncombe - Godalming - Milford - Witley - Chiddingfold. |
| 571 | 1/11/87 | Service 571 diverted at Milford to double-run to Milford Station and Milford Hospital. |
| 571 | 23/10/88 | Service 571 withdrawn on re-tendering, new contract awarded to Alder Valley. |

## 9. Reigate - Redhill via Meadvale or Batts Hill - Routes 547 and 587

| | | |
|---|---|---|
| 547 | 27/10/86 | New Monday to Saturday service ("The Hobbit") operated under contract to Surrey C.C.: Reigate - Meadvale - Earlswood - Redhill. One morning peak journey operated from Whitebushes Estate to Redhill via East Surrey Hospital and Earlswood. |

| | | |
|---|---|---|
| 587 | 27/10/86 | New Monday to Saturday service ("The Hobbit") operated under contract to Surrey C.C.: Reigate - Batts Hill - Redhill. |
| 547 | 22/8/88 | Service 547 diverted in Earlswood via Emlyn Road and Brambletye Park Road. |

## B. Routes Primarily in West Sussex operated by Tillingbourne Bus Co. Ltd. or Tillingbourne (Sussex) Ltd.

### 1. Horsham - Holbrook - Rusper - Lambs Green - Routes 451, 452, 51, 52, 61. (Sussex)

| | | |
|---|---|---|
| 451 | 17/4/72 | Acquisition of North Downs Rural Transport route 851. Re-numbered 451: Horsham - Roffey Corner - Colgate - Faygate - Lambs Green - Rusper - Holbrook - Pondtail Road - Horsham (Monday to Saturday). Also local journeys: Horsham - North Heath Lane - Holbrook - Pondtail Road - Horsham. Also one Monday to Friday journey: Horsham - Broadbridge Heath - Warnham. |
| 451 | 2/75 | Garage journeys between Ewhurst and Rusper via Forest Green - Ockley - Capel. |
| 451 | 6/9/76 | Main service diverted via North Heath Lane instead of Pondtail Road. Warnham journey diverted via North Heath Lane - Holbrook - Warnham Station. Schoolday journeys to Forest and Millais Schools in Horsham. |
| 451 | 29/1/79 | Route 451 revised: Horsham - Pondtail Road - Holbrook - North Heath Lane - Horsham, with certain journeys running: Horsham - North Heath Lane - Holbrook - Rusper - Lambs Green. |
| 452 | 24/9/79 | Lambs Green section of route re-numbered as service 452. |
| 451 | 24/9/79 | Improved frequency on service 451. Last Monday to Friday journey operated by London Country Bus Services. |
| 451 | 3/3/80 | Schoolday journeys on service 451: Kingsfold - Northlands - Warnham - Langhurst Wood Road - Holbrook to Horsham Schools. |
| 452 | 22/7/80 | Service 452 extended on Tuesdays and Fridays from Lambs Green to Ifield Wood - Ifield - Crawley. |
| 451 | 31/8/80 | London Country journey on service 451 withdrawn. |
| 452 | 1/6/81 | Service 452 withdrawn off-peak on Mondays, Wednesdays and Thursdays. Also Rusper - Lambs Green section withdrawn on Saturdays. |
| 451 | 5/7/82 | Service 451 revised: Horsham - North Heath Lane - Coltsfoot Drive - Brook Road - Chennells Brook - Holbrook - North Heath Lane - Horsham (Monday to Saturday). |
| 452 | 5/7/82 | Service 452 revised: Horsham - Pondtail Road - Holbrook - Chennells Brook - Rusper - Lambs Green (Monday to Friday), extended on Fridays to Ifield Wood - Ifield Crawley. Also Monday to Friday local journeys: Horsham - North Heath Lane - Holbrook - Pondtail Road - Horsham. |
| 452 | 6/6/83 | Service 452 curtailed at Lambs Green and revised to run peak hours only, except Tuesdays and Fridays. Diverted via North Heath Lane instead of Pondtail Road. |
| 51 | 14/4/85 | Service 451 re-numbered as route 51 |
| 52 | 14/4/85 | Service 452 re-numbered as route 52 |
| 52 | 27/10/86 | Service 52 reduced to Tuesday and Friday shopping trips. Routed via Pondtail Road instead of North Heath Lane and operated under contract to West Sussex County Council. |
| 51 | 24/8/87 | Some journeys on service 51 diverted via Foundry Lane between Horsham Station and North Heath Lane. |
| 51 | 20/2/89 | Journeys via Foundry Lane reduced to operate Monday to Friday peak hours only. |
| 52 | 20/2/89 | Service 52 revised to operate: Horsham - Roffey Corner - Colgate - Faygate - Lambs Green - Rusper - Chennells Brook - Holbrook - Pondtail Road - Horsham (Tuesdays, Fridays and Saturdays). Also, afternoon journey on schooldays: Horsham - Holbrook - Rusper - Newdigate. |
| 61 | 20/2/89 | New Monday to Friday service operated as route 61: Horsham - Pondtail Road - Holbrook - North Heath Lane - Wimblehurst Road - North Parade - Horsham. |

### 2. Ewhurst - Chichester via Cranleigh, Alfold, Plaistow and Petworth - Route 454

| | | |
|---|---|---|
| 454 | 6/4/77 | New service 454 on first Wednesday in each month: Ewhurst - Cranleigh - Hazelwood - Alfold Crossways - Alfold - Loxwood - Ifold - Plaistow - Mackerels Common - Petworth - Chichester. |
| 454 | 5/10/77 | Commenced running also on third Wednesday in each month. |
| 454 | 5/1/79 | Reduced to run on first Wednesday in each month only, but every Wednesday during August 1979. |
| 454 | 3/9/80 | Service 454 withdrawn, replaced by London Country 854. |

### 3. Dunsfold - Horsham via Plaistow and Alfold - Route 446

| | | |
|---|---|---|
| 446 | 5/9/80 | New Friday service 446: Dunsfold - Durfold Wood - Plaistow - Ifold - Loxwood - Alfold - Alfold Crossways - Tismans Common - Horsham. |
| 446 | 10/8/81 | Restriction on carriage of local passengers Tismans Common to Horsham removed. Bucks Green, Clemsfold, Broadbridge Heath also served. |
| 446 | 2/7/82 | Service 446 withdrawn. |

### 4. Horsham - Steyning/Brighton via Southwater and Partridge Green - Route 453 (Sussex)

| | | |
|---|---|---|
| 453 | 1/6/81 | New service 453 operated on Mondays, Wednesdays and Thursdays: Horsham - Southwater - Buckbarn - West Grinstead - Partridge Green - Ashurst - Steyning. |
| 453 | 6/7/82 | Revised to operate on Tuesdays only and extended from Steyning to Bramber - Upper Beeding - Southwick - Hove Brighton. |
| 453 | 31/5/83 | Service 453 withdrawn. |

### 5. Cranleigh - Horsham/Brighton via Southwater and Poynings - Routes 454, 457 and 54 (Sussex)

| | | |
|---|---|---|
| 454 | 2/6/81 | New service 454 operated on Tuesdays: Ewhurst - Cranleigh - Ellens Green - Rudgwick - Broadbridge Heath - Horsham - Southwater - Buckbarn - West Grinstead - Partridge Green - Shermanbury - Henfield - Small Dole - Edburton - Fulking - Poynings - Pyecombe - Patcham - Brighton. |
| 454 | 6/7/82 | Revised to operate: Gomshall - Shere (during school holidays) - Albury - Chilworth - Wonersh - Shamley Green - Cranleigh - Hazelwood - Alfold Crossways - Alfold - Loxwood - Ifold - Plaistow - Ifold - Loxwood - Tismans Common - Bucks Green - Broadbridge Heath - Horsham, then as before to Brighton. Operated also on Fridays between Cranleigh and Horsham. |
| 454 | 10/9/82 | Curtailed on Fridays to operate between Alfold Crossways and Horsham. |
| 457 | 21/12/82 | New service 457 on Tuesdays during school holidays: Cranleigh - Ewhurst - Forest Green - Mayes Green - Walliswood - Oakwoodhill - Ockley - Kennels Cross Roads - Northlands - Warnham - Horsham (connecting with service 454 to Brighton). |
| 457 | 15/2/83 | Service 457 withdrawn. |
| 454 | 7/6/83 | Service 454 revised on Tuesdays to commence from Chilworth (schooldays only) or Cranleigh (school holidays). Extended from Brighton to Worthing. |
| 454 | 5/9/83 | Additional schoolday journeys: Alfold Crossways - Alfold - Loxwood - Tismans Common - Bucks Green - Broadbridge Heath - Horsham (afternoon journey ran through to Cranleigh). Morning journey also ran during school holidays and on Saturdays between Bucks Green and Horsham. |
| 454 | 13/12/83 | Diverted via Littleworth between West Grinstead and Partridge Green. |
| 454 | 3/7/84 | Tuesday service withdrawn. Afternoon schoolday journey curtailed at Alfold Crossways. |
| 54 | 14/4/85 | Service 454 re-numbered as route 54. Afternoon schoolday and Friday shoppers journeys extended from Alfold Crossways to Cranleigh. |
| 54 | 25/7/86 | Schoolday and peak hour journeys withdrawn. |

| | | |
|---|---|---|
| 54 | 31/10/86 | Operated under contract to West Sussex County Council. |

**6. Cranleigh - Arundel & Arundel - Burpham via Alfold and Pulborough - Routes 455 and 456**

| | | |
|---|---|---|
| 455 | 10/9/82 | New Friday service: Cranleigh - Hazelwood - Alfold Crossways - Alfold - Loxwood - Roundstreet Common - Newpound - Adversane - Pulborough - Coldwaltham - Watersfield - Bury - Amberley - Houghton - Whiteways Lodge - Arundel. |
| 456 | 10/9/82 | New Friday service: Burpham - Wepham Corner - Warningcamp Turn - Arundel. |
| 455<br>456 | 25/2/83 | Services 455 and 456 withdrawn. |

**7. Cranleigh - Forest Green/Horsham via Walliswood and Warnham - Routes 450, 50 and 53**

| | | |
|---|---|---|
| 450 | 6/6/83 | New service 450 to replace parts of routes 446 and 452: Cranleigh - Ewhurst Green - Walliswood - Oakwoodhill - Kennels Cross Roads - Northlands - Warnham - Broadbridge Heath - Horsham (Monday to Friday peak hours). Also Shoppers journeys serving Ewhurst (Tuesdays and Fridays), Ockley and Rowhook (Tuesdays, Fridays and Saturdays). Also Monday to Friday journeys: Horsham - Pondtail Road - Warnham Station - Warnham - Broadbridge Heath - Horsham. Also Thursday journey: Ockley - Oakwoodhill - Walliswood - Mayes Green - Forest Green (connecting with service 446 to Guildford). |
| 450 | 5/7/84 | Ockley Thursday journey withdrawn. |
| 50<br>53 | 14/4/85 | Service 450 re-numbered as route 50. Friday shoppers journey withdrawn. Tuesday shoppers journey revised to commence from Forest Green instead of Cranleigh. Horsham - Warnham circulars re-numbered as route 50 (via Broadbridge Heath) and 53 (via Warnham Station). |
| 50<br>53 | 27/10/86 | Rowhook diversion reduced to operate on Tuesdays only (under contract to West Sussex County Council). Additional Monday to Saturday off-peak journeys Walliswood - Horsham. Evening peak journey Horsham - Cranleigh re-numbered 53 and diverted between Horsham and Warnham via North Heath Lane - Holbrook - Warnham Station. Horsham - Warnham circulars via Pondtail Road withdrawn. |
| 53 | 24/8/87 | Monday to Friday service 53 journey diverted via Broadbridge Heath as service 50, but still as 53 on Saturdays. |
| 50 | 3/9/87 | Off-peak buses revised to operate: Cranleigh (Saturdays) - or Forest Green (Tuesdays) - Walliswood - Oakwoodhill (Tuesdays, Fridays and Saturdays) - Ockley (Tuesdays and Saturdays) - Rowhook (Tuesdays) - Northlands (Tuesdays, Fridays and Saturdays) - Warnham - Broadbridge Heath - Horsham (Monday to Saturday). |
| 50 | 20/2/89 | Additional Monday to Saturday journeys between Horsham and Warnham. Diverted via Lower Broadbridge. Journeys at Warnham terminate via Bell Road, Dorking Road and School Hill. Afternoon journey on schooldays: Horsham - Warnham - Northlands - Kingsfold - Dorking Station. One Monday to Friday afternoon journey diverted between Northlands and Broadbridge Heath via Clemsfold. |
| 50 | 28/10/89 | Off-peak Saturday service 50 curtailed to operate Walliswood - Horsham. |

**8. Horsham - Coolham via Christs Hospital, Barns Green and Brooks Green - Route 55 (Sussex)**

| | | |
|---|---|---|
| 55 | 27/10/86 | New Monday to Saturday service operated under contract to West Sussex County Council: Horsham - Christs Hospital - Itchingfield - Barns Green - Brooks Green. Extended Monday to Friday peak hours to Coolham - Billingshurst - Newpound - Roundstreet Common - Loxwood - Alfold - Alfold Crossways. Diverted via Needles Estate in Horsham on Tuesdays, Fridays and Saturdays. |
| 55 | 24/8/87 | Tuesdays and Fridays off-peak journeys extended from Brooks Green to Coolham. Needles Estate diversion withdrawn. |
| 55 | 18/2/89 | Service 55 withdrawn and replaced by London & Country. |

### 9. Horsham - Crawley via Colgate and Pease Pottage. - Route 56 (Sussex)

| | | |
|---|---|---|
| 56 | 28/10/86 | New Tuesday, Thursday and Saturday service operated under contract to West Sussex County Council: Horsham - Roffey Corner - Colgate - Pease Pottage - Southgate - Crawley. On Thursdays, commenced at Warnham and ran via Broadbridge Heath to Horsham and Crawley. |
| 56 | 27/1/87 | Colgate - Crawley section reduced to operate on Thursdays only. |
| 56 | 27/8/87 | Thursday journey revised to commence from Southwater and ran via Timber Mill and Cedar Drive to Horsham. |
| 56 | 20/2/89 | Revised to operate on Thursdays only between Horsham and Crawley. Some journeys diverted between Roffey Corner and Crawley via Faygate. |

### 10. Horsham - Oakhill Estate - Route 292 (Sussex)

| | | |
|---|---|---|
| 292 | 31/1/87 | New temporary Saturday service operated under contract to West Sussex County Council: Horsham (Carfax) - Station - Depot Road - Compton's Lane - Oakhill - Station - Horsham (Carfax). |
| 292 | 14/2/87 | Service 292 withdrawn and replaced by London Country South West Minibus route. |

### 11. Horsham - Guildford via Billingshurst, Plaistow and Godalming - Route 60 (Sussex)

| | | |
|---|---|---|
| 60 | 17/6/87 | New Wednesdays service: Horsham - Christ's Hospital - Itchingfield - Barns Green - Billingshurst - Wisborough Green - Kirdford - Mackerels Common - Plaistow - Durfold Wood - Dunsfold - Loxhill - Hascombe - Winkworth - Busbridge - Godalming - Guildford. |
| 60 | 15/2/89 | Service 60 withdrawn. |

### 12. Alfold/Storrington - Horsham via Billingshurst and Slinfold - Routes 57, 58 and 59 (Sussex)

| | | |
|---|---|---|
| 57 | 20/2/89 | New Monday to Friday peak hours service operated as route 57: Alfold Crossways - Alfold - Loxwood - Kirdford - Wisborough Green - Forge Way - Parbrook - Billingshurst - Five Oaks - Slinfold - Broadbridge Heath - Horsham. |
| 58 | 20/2/89 | New Monday to Friday service operated as route 58: Horsham - Broadbridge Heath - Slinfold - Five Oaks - Billingshurst - Parbrook . Extended on Mondays, Wednesdays and Fridays to Forge Way and Wisborough Green. One afternoon journey between Five Oaks and Broadbridge Heath via Toat Hill. |
| 59 | 20/2/89 | New Tuesdays and Thursdays service operated as route 59: Horsham - Broadbridge Heath - Slinfold - Five Oaks - Billingshurst - Parbrook - Adversane - Pulborough - Marehill - West Chiltington Common - Storrington. |
| All | 28/4/89 | Services 57, 58 and 59 withdrawn, similar routes continued to be operated by Sussex Bus under contract to West Sussex County Council. |

## C. Routes Primarily Operated in London by Tillingbourne Greater London Tillingbourne (Metropolitan) Ltd

### 1. Croydon - Orpington via Addington, Forestdale and Locks Bottom. Routes 855, 353, 355 and 357

| | | |
|---|---|---|
| 855 | 2/3/81 | New service operated as route 855 replacing Orpington and District on Monday to Friday peak hours only: East Croydon - Addington - Forestdale. |
| 353 | 21/4/81 | New service on Monday to Friday peak hours operated as route 353: East Croydon - Addington - Coney Hall - Keston Mark - Locks Bottom - Orpington. |

| | | |
|---|---|---|
| 355 | 21/4/81 | New service replacing route 855 on Monday to Friday peak hours operating as route 355: East Croydon - Addington - Forestdale. |
| 357 | 21/4/81 | New service on Monday to Saturday operating as route 357: East Croydon - Addington - Forestdale - Coney Hall - Keston Mark - Locks Bottom - Orpington. |
| All | 9/11/81 | Routes extended during shopping hours from East Croydon to Croydon (Fairfield Halls). |
| All | 24/9/83 | All routes acquired by Metrobus Ltd. |

### 2. Orpington - Brighton via Forestdale and Coulsdon - Route 350

| | | |
|---|---|---|
| 350 | 1/5/82 | New Summer Saturday, Sunday and Bank Holiday express service: Ramsden Estate - Orpington - Locks Bottom - Keston Mark - Coney Hall - New Addington - Forestdale - Selsdon - Sanderstead - Purley - Coulsdon - Brighton. |
| 350 | 1/5/83 | Stops introduced at Hickstead and Preston Park. |
| 350 | 2/8/83 | Also operated on Tuesdays and Thursdays in August. |
| 350 | 24/9/83 | Route acquired by Metrobus Ltd. |

### 3. Sanderstead - Bromley via Selsdon, Forestdale and New Addington - Route 354

| | | |
|---|---|---|
| 354 | 4/5/82 | New Monday to Friday service operated as route 354: Sanderstead - Selsdon - Forestdale - New Addington - Bromley. |
| 354 | 22/11/82 | Diverted via Hayes - Bourne Vale - Pickhurst Park. |
| 354 | 24/9/83 | Route acquired by Metrobus Ltd. |

## D. Routes Primarily in Hampshire Operated by Tillingbourne Bus Co. Tillingbourne (Hampshire) Ltd.

### New network of "Hobbit" minibus services operated under contract to Hampshire County Council

| | | |
|---|---|---|
| F12 | 2/1/90 | Crookham (The Verne) - Wyvern Inn - Fleet - Cove - Farnborough - North Camp - Aldershot (Monday to Friday morning peak hours in this direction only). |
| F13 | 2/1/90 | Farnborough - Cove - Fleet - Crookham (The Verne) - Quetta Park (Monday to Saturday). |
| F14 | 2/1/90 | Fleet - Humphrey Park or Crookham Village - Wyvern Inn - Crookham (The Verne) (Monday to Saturday). |
| F15 | 2/1/90 | Fleet - Kings Road - Pondtail - Velmead Road - Fleet (Monday to Saturday). |
| F16 | 2/1/90 | Fleet - Kings Road - Pondtail - Aldershot Road - Fleet (Monday to Saturday). |
| F17 | 2/1/90 | Farnborough - Cove - Ancells Farm - Fleet (Monday to Saturday). |
| F25 | 2/1/90 | Farnborough - Southwood Estate - Pyestock Estate (Monday to Saturday). |
| F26 | 2/1/90 | Farnborough - Farnborough Street - Ship Inn (Monday to Saturday). |
| F36 | 2/1/90 | Farnborough - Cove - Minley Estate - Guillemont Fields (Monday to Saturday). |
| F37 | 2/1/90 | Farnborough - Rafborough (Monday to Saturday). |
| F38 | 2/1/90 | Yateley - Vigo Lane - Handford Lane - Fleet Station (Monday to Friday, peak hours only). |

TILLINGBOURNE GROUP OF COMPANIES - HISTORICAL FLEET LIST

| Fleet No. | Reg. No. | Chassis | Body | Seating | Date Purchased | Date Withdrawn | Former Owner | Subsequent Owner | Note |
|---|---|---|---|---|---|---|---|---|---|
| | PD 13XX | Chevrolet | ? | B14F | /24 | ? | - | Not traced | |
| | PE 1279 | Overland | ? | B14F | /25 | ? | - | Not traced | |
| | PH 4967 | Chevrolet | ? | B14F | /27 | ? | - | Branton, Felixstowe | |
| | PH 8502 | Chevrolet | ? | B14F | /27 | 3/28 | - | Destroyed by fire | |
| | PH 8654 | Chevrolet | ? | B14F | /27 | 3/28 | - | Destroyed by fire | |
| | PH 8824 | Chevrolet | ? | B14F | /28 | 3/28 | - | Destroyed by fire | |
| | UO 9841 | Thornycroft A2 | Mumford | B20F | /28 | 4/37 | Geddes, Brixham | Newbury & District, Newbury | |
| | UP 3203 | Thornycroft A6 | ? | ? | /28 | 6/34 | Thornycroft (Demonstrator) | Showman | |
| | UP 5280 | Dennis G | ? | B18F | /28 | ? | Not traced | Not traced | |
| | YB 9506 | Dennis G | ? | B18F | /28 | 1/35 | Not traced | Not traced | |
| | PK 5889 | Dennis G | ? | B18F | /29 | 1/35 | - | Not traced | |
| 2 | PG 8268 | Thornycroft A2 | Short | B18F | /30 | 11/38 | - | Scrapped | |
| 3 | PL 5339 | Dennis GL | Dennis | B20F | /31 | 1/36 | - | Not traced | |
| 4 | BPL 208 | Thornycroft Handy | Thurgood | B20F | 11/34 | 11/38 | - | Not traced | |
| 5 | DPC 200 | Thornycroft Handy | Waveney | B20F | 11/35 | /45 | - | Not traced | 1 |
| 6 | EPH 686 | Thornycroft Dainty | Thurgood | B20F | 1/37 | 12/50 | - | Not traced | |
| 7 | GPB 957 | Thornycroft Dainty | Waveney | B20F | 1/38 | 10/51 | - | Guide Dogs for Blind Assoc. | |
| 8 | HPL 265 | Thornycroft Nippy | Waveney | B20F | 5/39 | 12/55 | - | Girl Guides, East Grinstead | |
| 9 | JPK 518 | Dodge RBF | Harrington | B20F | /42 | /43 | ? , Isle of Man | Bere Regis & District | |
| 10 | JPL 88 | Bedford OWB | Duple | UB32F | 1/43 | 5/53 | - | Racing Car Transporter | 2 |
| 11 | KPE 425 | Thornycroft Nippy | Thurgood | B20F | 2/46 | 5/56 | - | Gillingham Co-op(Mob. Shop) | |
| | JXH 720 | Bedford OB | Pearson | C26F | 1/50 | 1/56 | Fallowfield & Britten, E8 | Sims & Russell, SW1(Contr.) | |
| | MNU 689 | Bedford OB | Woodall Nicholson | B29F | 1/51 | /60 | Booth & Fisher, Halfway | Caravan | |
| | NGX 513 | Austin CXB | Pearson | C26F | 1/53 | 1/58 | Manchester Co-op (Lorry) | Miles Aircraft, Shoreham | |
| | EKU 810 | Austin K4VT | Plaxton | B29F | 1/55 | /60 | Short, Swansea | Hewitt, Cranleigh(Mob.Shop) | |
| | JLG 991 | Bedford OB | Plaxton | FC29F | 11/55 | /60 | Holder, SE8 | Scrapped | |
| | JTB 262 | Bedford OB | Plaxton | FC30F | 11/56 | /62 | Cornish, Dewton | Stockcar Trans., Farncombe | |
| | MPE 296 | Austin CXB | Plaxton | C29F | 10/57 | 4/63 | Cocke, Stoughton | ? , Newbury | |
| | OEV 889 | Bedford OB | Duple Vista | C29F | 7/59 | 7/63 | Lancing & Bagnall,B'stoke | Mob. Shop, Godalming | |
| | EUX 7 | Bedford OB | Duple Vista | C29F | 9/59 | 9/63 | Harling, SE1 | Cruse, Warminster | |
| | TMY 26 | Bedford OB | Duple Vista | C29F | 1/60 | 9/63 | Beach, Staines | Brown, Guildford | |
| | GHS 721 | Bedford SBG | Burlingham Seagull | C35F | 7/60 | 4/63 | Coffen, New Milton | Geen, South Molton | |
| | ETL 221 | Bedford OB | Plaxton | C29F | 6/61 | 3/63 | Taylor, Marlow | Farmer, Swanley | |

| | | | | | | | | | |
|---|---|---|---|---|---|---|---|---|---|
| 1 | MXX 301 | Guy Special NVLLP | ECW | B26F | 3/63 | 2/69 | London Transport | Trice, Chilworth(Preserved) | |
| 3 | MXX 303 | Guy Special NVLLP | ECW | B26F | 3/63 | 6/71 | London Transport | Purley Car Co., Warlingham | |
| 8 | MXX 304 | Guy Special NVLLP | ECW | B26F | 3/63 | 5/71 | London Transport | Scrapyard, Alfold | |
| 7 | MXX 367 | Guy Special NVLLP | ECW | B26F | 5/63 | 7/69 | London Transport | Gould, London (Preserved) | |
| 2 | MXX 369 | Guy Special NVLLP | ECW | B26F | 5/63 | 9/65 | London Transport | Scrapped after accident | |
| 4 | MXX 384 | Guy Special NVLLP | ECW | B26F | 3/64 | 7/70 | London Transport | Watson, Wootton Bridge IOW | |
| 6 | MXX 376 | Guy Special NVLLP | ECW | B26F | 5/64 | 4/71 | London Transport | Mobile Caravan | |
| 5 | MXX 325 | Guy Special NVLLP | ECW | B26F | 10/64 | 7/68 | London Transport | Scrapped | |
| 5 | MXX 324 | Guy Special NVLLP | ECW | B26F | 7/68 | 5/71 | London Fire Brigade | Scrapyard, Alfold | |
| | MXX 359 | Guy Special NVLLP | ECW | B26F | 12/69 | 12/69 | London Transport | Scrapped | 3 |
| 2 | MXX 382 | Guy Special NVLLP | ECW | B26F | 1/70 | 3/72 | LT Civil Defence Vehicle | Filling Station, Gt.Sutton | 4 |
| | JUO 982 | Bristol LL6B | ECW | FB39F | 10/70 | 12/71 | Western National | Scout Troop, Milford | |
| | HBL 70 | Bristol KSW6B | ECW | L55R | 12/70 | 4/71 | Thames Valley | Harrimonde, Brighton | |
| | MXX 314 | Guy Special NVLLP | ECW | B26F | 12/70 | 10/71 | London Country | Ballets Minerva, Wembley | |
| | NNY 55 | Ley'd Tiger Cub PSUC1/1 | Weymann | B44F | 1/71 | 4/71 | Creamline, Tonmawr | Martin, Weaverham (Dealer) | |
| 5 | TVF 537 | Bristol SC4LK | ECW | B35F | 2/71 | 11/71 | Eastern Counties | Scrapped | |
| 6 | 6560 AH | Bristol SC4LK | ECW | B35F | 2/71 | 5/72 | Eastern Counties | Sykes, Barnsley (Dealer) | |
| 7 | 790 EFM | Bristol SC4LK | ECW | B35F | 4/71 | 6/72 | Crosville | Sykes, Barnsley (Dealer) | |
| | 170 BUP | Albion Aberdonian MR11L | Willowbrook | B45F | 4/71 | 7/71 | Venture, Consett | Martin,Weaverham (Dealer) | |
| | MXX 364 | Guy Special NVLLP | ECW | B26F | 4/71 | 10/72 | London Country | Lines,Upp.Norwood(Presvd) | |
| C1 | 645 WKX | AEC Reliance 4MU3RA | Harrington | C51F | 6/71 | 1/74 | Keith, Aylesbury | Gath, Thornhill | |
| | 2521 WE | AEC Bridgemaster B3RA | Park Royal | H76R | 6/71 | ?/71 | Sheffield | Godwin, Carlton (Dealer) | |
| | VJF 214 | AEC Bridgemaster B3RA | Park Royal | H72R | 6/71 | 9/71 | Leicester City Transport | Scutt, Owston Ferry | 5 |
| | MOD 952 | Bristol LS5G | ECW | B41F | 6/71 | 7/71 | Western National | Wilder, Feltham | |
| | MOD 966 | Bristol LS5G | ECW | B41F | 6/71 | 1/72 | Western National | Scrapped | |
| | MOD 954 | Bristol LS5G | ECW | B41F | 7/71 | 10/71 | Western National | North Downs, Forest Green | |
| | KDD 275 E | Daimler Roadliner SRC6 | Plaxton Panorama | C47F | 7/71 | 11/73 | Black & White, Cheltenham | Phillips, London Colney | |
| | LTA 988 | Bristol LS5G | ECW | B41F | 8/71 | 1/72 | Western National | Hopkins, Tonna | |
| | FPO 426 H | Ford Transit | Strachans | B16F | 9/71 | 11/71 | North Downs, Forest Green | Chivers, Elstead | |
| | PHW 931 | Bristol LS5G | ECW | B41F | 10/71 | 12/71 | Thames Valley | Scrapped | |
| | NLE 595 | AEC Regal IV RF | Metro Cammell | B39F | 9/71 | 10/73 | London Country | Matthew Arnold Sch.,Staines | |
| | LWN 52 | Bristol Lodekka LD6B | ECW | H60RD | 12/71 | 12/72 | Thames Valley | Jefferys, Grayshott | |
| | YUE 163 | Bedford SB3 | Plaxton Embassy | C41F | 1/72 | 8/72 | Chivers, Elstead | Not traced | |
| | 3255 PJ | Bedford VAS1 | Marshall | B29F | 1/72 | 6/72 | North Downs, Forest Green | Chivers, Elstead | |
| | 417 HDV | Bristol SUL4A | ECW | B36F | 2/72 | 6/75 | Western National | Bickers, Coddenham | |
| | 347 EDV | Bristol SUL4A | ECW | B36F | 4/72 | 12/73 | Western National | Not traced | |
| | MAX 133 | Bristol LS6G | ECW | C39F | 5/72 | 7/72 | Gosport & Fareham | Martin, Weaverham (Dealer) | |
| | MAX 134 | Bristol LS6G | ECW | C39F | 5/72 | 2/73 | Gosport & Fareham | Martin, Weaverham (Dealer) | |
| | SOU 454 | Dennis Loline 1 | East Lancs | H68RD | 5/72 | 9/72 | Stringer, Ampthill | School, Brighton area | |
| | LPD 12 K | Bedford YRQ | Willowbrook | B47F | 6/72 | 5/79 | - | McCann, Forest Green | |

| | | | | | | | | |
|---|---|---|---|---|---|---|---|---|
| NLE 680 | AEC Regal IV RF | Metro Cammell | B39F | 7/72 | 4/73 | London Country | Scrapped | 5 |
| NLE 699 | AEC Regal IV RF | Metro Cammell | B39F | 7/72 | 11/73 | London Country | Matthew Arnold Sch.,Staines | |
| 355 EDV | Bristol SUL4A | ECW | B36F | 8/72 | 6/73 | Western National | Hutton Wandesley Farmers | |
| MLL 770 | AEC Regal IV RF | Metro Cammell | B39F | 12/72 | 6/73 | London Country | Not traced | 5 |
| MLL 791 | AEC Regal IV RF | Metro Cammell | B37F | 12/72 | 3/73 | London Country | Wylde & Edwards, Orpington | 5 |
| NPH 33 L | Ley'd Leopard PSU3B/4R | Willowbrook Exp'way | C51F | 1/73 | 4/76 | - | Sherwood Hosp., Nottingham | |
| 6108 WU | Ley'd Tiger Cub PSUC1/2 | Duple Donnington | DP41F | 6/73 | 6/74 | Pennine, Gargrave | Bleanch, Hetton Le Hole | |
| 9712 WX | Ley'd Tiger Cub PSUC1/2 | Duple Donnington | DP41F | 6/73 | 12/75 | Pennine, Gargrave | Worldwide(Scotland),Lanark | * |
| 318 EDV | Bristol SUL4A | ECW | B36F | 8/73 | 3/75 | Gosport & Fareham | Godwin, Carlton (Scrap) | 3 |
| 554 GXX | AEC Reliance 2MU4RA | Harrington | C41F | 10/73 | 10/74 | Timpson, Catford | Horlock, Northfleet | |
| 269 KTA | Bristol SUL4A | ECW | DP33F | 11/73 | 12/74 | Western National | Bickers, Coddenham | * |
| PWY 595 M | Bedford YRT | Duple Dominant | C53F | 1/74 | 6/80 | - | Valeside, London NW10 | |
| VCH 172 | Ley'd Tiger Cub PSUC1/2 | Willowbrook | DP41F | 5/74 | 8/75 | Ford, Gunnislake | Kendall & Retallick, G'ford | |
| GPA 846 N | Bedford YRQ | Plaxton Derwent | B45F | 10/74 | 11/81 | - | Banstead Coaches | |
| 6217 PU | Ley'd Tiger Cub PSUC1/2 | Duple Donnington | C41F | 12/74 | 12/75 | Thomas, West Ewell | Hargreaves, Newbury | * |
| 240 CWY | Leyland Leopard L2 | Roe | B47F | 8/75 | 10/77 | Pennine, Gargrave | Berresford, Cheddleton | |
| LWU 499 D | Leyland Leopard PSU4/3R | Roe | B49F | 9/75 | 5/78 | Pennine, Gargrave | Yeates (Dealer) | |
| LPE 42 P | Bedford YRQ | Plaxton Supreme | C45F | 12/75 | 4/81 | - | Lefkaritis, Cyprus | * |
| MPE 248 P | Bedford YRQ | Plaxton Derwent | B45F | 4/76 | 11/82 | - | Farhham Coaches,Wrecclesham | |
| ACU 303 C | Leyland Leopard PSU3/3R | Harrington | C51F | 9/76 | 4/77 | Browne, Smallfield | Munden, Bristol | |
| SPA 192 R | Bedford YMT | Plaxton Supreme | C53F | 5/77 | 9/83 | - | Metrobus, Orpington | ** |
| KWW 901 K | Seddon Pennine IV | Seddon | B56F | 8/77 | 9/77 | Morris, Bromyard | Yeates (Dealer) | |
| TRN 769 | Ley'd Leopard PSU3/1RT | Marshall | DP49F | 10/77 | 12/78 | Ribble | Knubley, Bruton | |
| GGR 344 N | Bedford YRQ | Willowbrook | B47F | 10/77 | 10/79 | Tyne & Wear PTE | McCann, Forest Green | |
| WPL 985 S | Bedford YLQ | Plaxton Supreme | C45F | 6/78 | 6/83 | - | Dorset County Council | |
| XPL 889 T | Bedford YMT | Duple Dominant | B61F | 9/78 | 9/83 | - | Metrobus, Orpington | * |
| GYA 737 T | Bedford CFS | Dormobile | 12 | 1/79 | 11/82 | - | Private owner, G'ford | |
| CPG 160 T | AEC Reliance 6U3ZR | Plaxton Supreme | C53F | 4/79 | 4/88 | - | Salmon, Guildford | |
| TYD 122 G | AEC Reliance 6MU3R | Willowbrook | B45F | 6/79 | 8/80 | H & C, South Petherton | Chiltern Queens, Woodcote | |
| EPH 27 V | Bedford YLQ | Duple Dominant | B52F | 8/79 | 10/84 | - | Semmence, Wymondham | |
| JTM 109 V | AEC Reliance 6U2R | Duple Dominant | B53F | 11/79 | 9/83 | - | Metrobus,Orpington (Leased) | * |
| CCG 550 V | Bedford YMT | Duple Dominant | B61F | 7/80 | 9/87 | - | Reynard Pullman, York | |
| UKX 150 J | AEC Reliance 6U2R | Plaxton Derwent | DP51F | 10/80 | 9/82 | Red Rover, Aylesbury | Morris, Bromyard | 6** |
| NDV 44 W | Bedford YMT | Duple Dominant | C53F | 12/80 | 4/82 | - | Evans, New Tredegar | |
| ODV 404 W | AEC Reliance 6U2R | Duple Dominant | C53F | 3/81 | 9/83 | - | Metrobus,Orpington (Leased) | ** |
| ODV 405 W | AEC Reliance 6U2R | Duple Dominant | C53F | 3/81 | 9/83 | - | Metrobus,Orpington (Leased) | ** |
| SKN 491 R | Bedford YMT | Willowbrook | B53F | 4/81 | 5/82 | Maidstone Borough Council | Bickers, Coddenham | * |
| SPT 647 V | Bedford YMT | Duple Dominant | B55F | 10/81 | 3/84 | Langley Park Motor Co. | Grenville, Camborne | |
| TTA 650 X | Dennis Lancet SD502 | Wadham Stringer | B52F | 11/81 | 1/88 | - | E Jones, Wrexham | |
| BYG 851 H | Bristol VRTSL6LX | ECW | H70F | 2/82 | 9/83 | West Yorkshire Road Car | Metrobus, Orpington | ** |

| | | | | | | | | |
|---|---|---|---|---|---|---|---|---|
| TPL 762 X | Ley'd Tiger TRBTL11/2R | Plaxton Supreme V | C53F | 4/82 | 9/84 | - | Pennine, Gargrave | |
| XTT 5 X | Dennis Lancet SD502 | Wadham Stringer | B52F | 6/82 | 1/88 | - | Reid, Bedford | |
| LPD 12 K | Bedford YRQ | Willowbrook | B47F | 10/82 | 11/82 | McCann, Forest Green | Yeates (Dealer) | 5 |
| KAP 20 L | Bedford YRT | P'ton Panorama Elite | C53F | 10/82 | 3/83 | McCann, Forest Green | McCann, Forest Green | |
| NMJ 279 V | Bedford YMT | Plaxton Supreme | C53F | 10/82 | 9/85 | McCann, Forest Green | Evans, New Tredegar | |
| BGR 631 W | Bedford YMT | Duple Dominant | B55F | 10/82 | 8/84 | Langley Park Motor Co. | Davies, Carmarthen | * |
| YFX 182 Y | Ford Transit | Yeates | 12 | 10/82 | 7/85 | - | Stevens, West Bromwich | |
| FOD 941 Y | Bedford YMT | Plaxton Bustler | B55F | 4/83 | 10/89 | - | Reynard Pullman, York | |
| FOD 942 Y | Dennis DorchesterSDA802 | Wadham Stringer | B61F | 7/83 | - | - | - | 7 |
| FOD 943 Y | Dennis DorchesterSDA802 | Wadham Stringer | B61F | 7/83 | - | - | - | 7 |
| 898 FUF | Albion Victor FT39AN | Reading | B36F | 7/83 | 6/85 | Lidstone,Leigh (Preserved) | Elliott & Young (Preserved) | |
| A 889 FPM | Bedford YMT | Plaxton Bustler | B55F | 3/84 | - | - | - | |
| B 877 OLJ | Ley'd Tiger TRCTL11/2R | Duple Dominant | B55F | 8/84 | - | - | - | |
| B 124 PEL | Bedford YNT | Plaxton Paramount | C53F | 10/84 | 11/88 | - | Reynard Pullman, York | |
| B 327 KPD | Bedford YMT | Plaxton Bustler | B53F | 11/84 | - | - | - | |
| UGB 12 R | AEC Reliance 6U3ZR | Duple Dominant | B53F | 3/85 | 12/85 | Hutchison, Overtown | Bailey, Folkestone | |
| UGB 14 R | AEC Reliance 6U3ZR | Duple Dominant | B53F | 3/85 | 9/85 | Hutchison, Overtown | Safeguard, Guildford | |
| B 49 TVR | Ford Transit | Dixon Lomas | B16F | 4/85 | 10/86 | - | Not traced | |
| JDE 189 X | Ley'd Tiger TRCTL11/2R | Duple Dominant | C53F | 7/85 | 12/86 | Silcox, Pembroke Dock | Vince, Burghclere | |
| JTM 109 V | AEC Reliance 6U2R | Duple Dominant | B53F | 9/85 | - | Returned from Metrobus | - | |
| C 195 WJT | Ley'd Tiger TRBTL11/2RP | Duple Dominant | B53F | 11/85 | - | - | - | |
| ABR 778 S | Ley'd Leopard PSU3E/4R | Plaxton Derwent | B63F | 10/86 | 7/87 | Rainbow, Westbury | Hunter, Seaton Delavel | |
| D 424 XPJ | Fiat Iveco 49.10 | Robin Hood | B21F | 10/86 | - | - | - | 13 |
| D 425 XPJ | Fiat Iveco 49.10 | Robin Hood | B21F | 10/86 | - | - | - | 13 |
| GRF 264 V | Ley'd Leopard PSU3E/4R | Duple Dominant | C53F | 12/86 | 8/88 | P.M.T. | Felix, Stanley | |
| D 917 GRU | Bedford YMT | Plaxton Derwent II | B53F | 3/87 | - | - | - | |
| D 918 GRU | Bedford YMT | Plaxton Derwent II | B53F | 3/87 | - | - | - | |
| AEF 992 Y | Ley'd Tiger TRCTL11/2R | Plaxton Paramount | C53F | 7/87 | - | BTS, Borehamwood | - | 8 |
| ODV 405 W | AEC Reliance 6U2R | Duple Dominant | C53F | 9/87 | 5/88 | Returned from Metrobus | Metrobus, Orpington | |
| E 215 MFX | Bedford YMT | Plaxton Derwent II | B53F | 9/87 | - | - | - | 9 |
| E 216 MFX | Bedford YMT | Plaxton Derwent II | B53F | 9/87 | - | - | - | |
| B 919 NPC | Bedford YMPS | Lex Maxeta | B37F | 11/87 | - | Alder Valley South | - | |
| LCY 298 X | Bedford YMQS | Lex Maxeta | B37F | 3/88 | 5/88 | Berks Bucks Bus Co. | Green, Kirkintilloch | |
| LCY 299 X | Bedford YMQS | Lex Maxeta | B37F | 3/88 | 10/89 | Berks Bucks Bus Co. | R & I Coaches, London W1 | |
| LCY 301 X | Bedford YMQS | Lex Maxeta | B37F | 3/88 | 10/89 | Berks Bucks Bus Co. | R & I Coaches, London W1 | |
| B 918 NPC | Bedford YMPS | Lex Maxeta | B37F | 3/88 | - | Berks Bucks Bus Co. | - | 10 |
| E 536 PRU | Dennis Javelin | Plaxton Paramount | C53F | 5/88 | - | - | - | |
| F 870 TLJ | Ley'd Tiger TRBTL11/2RP | Plaxton Derwent II | B54F | 8/88 | - | - | - | |
| A 339 HNR | Volvo B10M | Plaxton Paramount | C53F | 8/88 | - | Woodstones, Kidderminster | - | |
| D 694 WAU | Bedford YMT | Plaxton Derwent II | B60F | 11/88 | - | Felix, Stanley | - | |

| | | | | | | | | |
|---|---|---|---|---|---|---|---|---|
| NUH 262 X | Volvo B10M | Plaxton Supreme V | C53F | 3/89 | - | James & Williams, Treorchy | - | 11 |
| G 401 DPD | Scania K93 | Plaxton Derwent II | B57F | 10/89 | - | - | - | 12 |
| G 407 DPD | Fiat Iveco 49.10 | Carlyle | DP25F | 11/89 | - | - | - | |
| G 402 DPD | Fiat Iveco 49.10 | Carlyle | B25F | 12/89 | - | - | - | 13 |
| G 403 DPD | Fiat Iveco 49.10 | Carlyle | B25F | 12/89 | - | - | - | 13 |
| G 404 DPD | Fiat Iveco 49.10 | Carlyle | B25F | 12/89 | - | - | - | 13 |
| G 405 DPD | Fiat Iveco 49.10 | Carlyle | B25F | 12/89 | - | - | - | 13 |
| G 406 DPD | Fiat Iveco 49.10 | Carlyle | B25F | 12/89 | - | - | - | 13 |
| G 810 DPH | Fiat Iveco 49.10 | Phoenix | B25F | 1/90 | - | - | - | 13 |

NOTES:

1 Renumbered 12
2 Initially ran as B20F
3 Acquired for spares
4 Acquired without seats
5 Not used in service
6 Reseated to B51F
7 Reseated 10/89 to B59F
8 Re-registered as TBC 658
9 Entered service 1/88
10 Not yet in service by 1/90 - Named "The Lord Hayman of Reigate"
11 Re-registered as 508 AHU
12 Entered service 12/89 - Named "The Lord Billy 'B'"
13 Minibuses for "Hobbit" services were named Jan 1990:
D 424 XPJ - "Will"
D 425 XPJ - "Rose"
G 402 DPD - "Sam"
G 403 DPD - "Pippin"
G 404 DPD - "Frodo"
G 405 DPD - "Bilbo"
G 406 DPD - "Merry"
G 810 DPH - "Fredegar" (Name not applied by Feb 1990)

* Licensed to Tillingbourne (Sussex) Ltd. } This differention only applicable until the
** Licensed to Tillingbourne (Metropolitan) Ltd. (From 7/81) } introduction of "license discs".

## Vehicles Operated in Service on Loan

| Reg.No. | Chassis Type | Body Type | Seating | Period Used | Owner |
|---|---|---|---|---|---|
| TYF 375 S | Ford Transit | Ford | 12 | 9/78 - 9/78 | T Brown |
| EYB 725 T | Bedford CFS | Dormobile | 12 | 9/78 - 1/79 | J Smith Car Hire |
| COO 242 T | Ford R1014 | Duple Dominant | B47F | 4/79 - 4/79 | Ford Motor Co.(Demonstrator) |
| NFR 558 T | Leyland National | Leyland | B51F | 8/79 - 8/79 | British Leyland (Demonstrator) |
| SWG 42 S | Bedford YMT | Plaxton Supreme | C53F | 1/85 - 2/85 | Yeates (Dealer) in livery of Angel Motors |
| AKK 171 T | Bedford YMT | Duple Dominant | B61F | 4/88 - 8/88 | Metrobus, Orpington |
| D 21 CTR | Bedford YMT | Wadham Stringer | B53F | 7/88 - 7/88 | Metrobus, Orpington |
| F 756 NPJ | Dennis Javelin | Duple 300 | B55F | 11/88 - 12/88 | Hestair Dennis (Demonstrator) |
| F 900 SMU | Leyland Swift | Wadham Stringer | B39F | 2/89 - 2/89 | Arlington (Demonstrator) |
| F 137 SPX | Dennis Javelin | Duple 300 | B63F | 6/89 - 6/89 | Hampshire Bus (Dennis Demonstrator) |
| G 221 EOA | Fiat Iveco 49.10 | Carlyle | B21F | 12/89 - 12/89 | Carlyle (Demonstrator) |
| F 368 RPO | Fiat Iveco 49.10 | Robin Hood | B23F | 12/89 - 1/90 | Phoenix Intl. (Demonstrator) |
| D 21 CTR | Bedford YMT | Wadham Stringer | B53F | 2/90 2/90 | Metrobus, Orpington |

TILLINGBOURNE VALLEY COACHES - HISTORICAL FLEET LIST

| Reg. No. | Chassis | Body | Seating | Date Purchased | Date Withdrawn | Former Owner | Subsequent Owner |
|---|---|---|---|---|---|---|---|
| PJ 717 | Bedford WLB | Duple | B20F | 10/31 | 10/36 | - | Bright, Chiddingfold |
| AMY 450 | Bedford WLB | Duple | B20F | 5/34 | 5/39 | Puttock, Guildford | Not traced |
| CPG 795 | Commer | Duple | B20F | 5/35 | 5/39 | - | Private owner, Middlesex |
| UC 4202 | Cadillac car | | 6 | 3/36 | 3/38 | Not traced | Not traced |
| EPL 870 | Bedford WTB | Thurgood | C26? | 3/37 | 2/50 | - | Not traced |
| KV 5 | ? | ? | ? | By 5/38 | 5/38 | Not traced | Not traced |
| HPJ 183 | Commer PLNF 5 | ? | C26? | 4/39 | 1/52 | - | Everyman, Maudlin |
| XG 5101 | Bedford WTB | Duple | C26? | ? | ? | Appleton, Middlesborough | Not traced |
| JPL 138 | Bedford OWB | Duple | UB32F | ?/43 | ? | - | ?, Glamorgan |
| KPA 477 | Bedford OWB | Duple | UB32F | ?/45 | ? | - | Not traced |
| KPE 959 | Bedford OB | Duple | B32F | ?/46 | 4/54 | - | Not traced |
| KPA 635 | Bedford OWB | Duple | UB30F | 5/49 | 2/51 | Hayter, Guildford | Not traced |
| MPE 296 | Austin CXB | Plaxton | C29F | 10/49 | 4/54 | Graves, Redhill | Rackcliffe, Guildford |
| MVX 881 | Maudslay Marathon II | Whitson | C35F | 2/50 | 4/54 | Universal, London N9 | Maryland, London E15 |

Notes: The standard enthusiasts format has been used to describe body types and seating capacities.

Prefix:

B - Single Decker Bus
C - Single Decker Coach
DP - Single Decker Dual Purpose Vehicle
FB - Single Decker Forward Control or Half Cab Bus with Flat Fronted Body
FC - Single Decker Forward Control or Half Cab Coach with Flat Fronted Body
UB - Single Decker Bus with Utility Body
L - Lowbridge Double Decker (with Sunken Side Gangway Upstairs)
H - Highbridge/Normal Height Double Decker

Figures: Seating Capacities as Stated

Suffix:

F - Front or Forward Entrance
R - Rear Entrance Open Platform
RD - Rear Entrance with Platform Doors

# ACKNOWLEDGEMENTS

As always with a book of this kind, the authors have received assistance from a considerable number of sources, and there is only space to mention some of them.

In no particular order, thanks must go to Barry LeJeune, whose thesis formed a firm base for further research of the formative years; Derek Trice and Trevor Brown, past and present proprietors respectively; Barry King, for the use of information contained in his 1974 Company history and other assistance; John Gaff, the current Traffic Manager of the Company; Roger Cox, for access to his 1975 paper on the operations of the Tillingbourne Bus Company; Jim Hatcher, former driver; Peter Larking, Managing Director of Metrobus Ltd. David Gray of the PSV Circle, who supplied details of the vehicles of the earlier years, whilst Stephen Morris allowed access to the Ian Allan Photographic Library. Assistance was also received from Brian Walter, Curator of the Omnibus Society's timetable collection; the staff of the local studies section of Guildford Library afforded access to microfilm records of the Surrey Advertiser newspaper; Shirley Corke of Surrey Record Office's Guildford Muniment Room for access to the minutes of the Guildford Town Watch Committee.

Additionally, thanks must go to those persons mentioned in the photographic credits for permission to use their work or to select from their collections. It has not been possible to trace all the sources and, where this is the case, they have been credited to "Authors Collection".

Special thanks must go to Vic and Barbara Mitchell of Middleton Press; to Deborah Goodridge who re-drew the maps and to Neil Stanyon for proof-reading. Finally, thanks to our wives who have allowed us to progress our long term interest in Tillingbourne into something more tangible.

# SELECTED BIBLIOGRAPHY

Durrant, Reg, King, John and Robbins, George. **East Surrey.**
(H J Publications 1974)

James, Lawrence. **Independent Bus Operators into Horsham.**
(Rochester Press 1983)

King, Barry. **Tillingbourne: 1924-1974.**
(Tillingbourne Bus Co.Ltd. 1974)

PSV Circle/Omnibus Society.
**The Small Stage Carriage Operators of the Metropolitan Traffic Area.**
(Fleet History PN2 1966)

Townsin, Alan.
**The Best of British Buses No.4 75 Years of Aldershot and District.**
(Transport Publishing Company 1981)

Hamshere, Norman and Sutton, John
**Happy Family - The Story of the Yellow Bus Services.**
(Published by Authors 1979)

**Buses** Magazine. (Ian Allan). Various issues, in particular:-

| | | |
|---|---|---|
| December 1973 | Buses to Coldharbour and Ockley | (L J Barry) |
| February 1975 | Co-ordination and Expansion | (B K Charles) |
| March 1983 | Dennis Lancet Test Drive | (S Morris) |
| June 1985 | The Shape of Things to Come | (L James) |
| " " | Independent View (S Morris Interview of B King) | |
| February 1987 | The State of Independence (Orpington Area) | (L James) |
| March 1987 | Post D-Day in Surrey | (L James) |

**The Omnibus Magazine** - Journal of the Omnibus Society: Spring 1985:
George Readings - Coach Pioneer(L James)

**Commericial Motor** 5 December 1981 Deep in the Heart of the "Environment".
(Noel Millier)
26 May 1984 Private Operators who believe in Service - Metrobus.
(Noel Millier)